S0-AXO-814

Gramley Library
Salem College
Winston-Salem, NC 27108

88-1931

ML
161
.6522
1980

MUSIC LITERATURE OUTLINES

SERIES V

CHAMBER MUSIC

FROM HAYDN TO BARTOK

by

Harold Gleason and Warren Becker

Second Edition

Frangipani Press

Division of T.I.S. Publications

Gramley Library
Salem College
Winston-Salem, NC 27108

SECOND EDITION
COPYRIGHT 1980

FRANGIPANI PRESS - TIS PUBLICATIONS
P.O. Box 1998
Bloomington, Indiana 47402
All rights reserved

Library of Congress Catalogue Card Number: 79-66417
ISBN 0-89917-267-9

CONTENTS

CHAMBER MUSIC FROM HAYDN TO BARTÓK

SALEM COLLEGE SCHOOL OF MUSIC

PREFACE TO THE SECOND EDITION

This edition of the *Music Literature Outlines, Series V,* is a revision of the first edition with the addition of the chamber music of Béla Bartók. It is intended to be an aid in the study of chamber music of selected representative European composers from Haydn to Bartók. The selected bibliographies at the end of each *Outline*, which include lists of books, periodical articles and music, have been revised and brought up to date. In general, the books and articles have been limited to those in the English language.

These *Outlines* provide a unique resource to the student, teacher, performer and listener whereby one may obtain a broad understanding and appreciation of chamber music. A study of the *Outlines* should be supplemented by performing the music, listening to recordings with the score and consulting the bibliographies. In the music bibliographies not only miniature study scores but also playing scores are listed, where available, although such lists are not necessarily exhaustive. References to the composers' complete works are included.

No attempt has been made to include all composers of chamber music, or all the chamber music of the composers represented. In general, the chamber music discussed is limited to works in the larger forms for ensembles of from three to six players, with emphasis on the string quartet. Sonatas for two instruments and works for various wind and brass ensembles are not included, except in the Catalogue of Chamber Music given for each composer. Contemporary American chamber music may be included in another series of outlines.

The writers are indebted to the late Verne W. Thompson for help in the preparation of the first edition of the *Outlines*, and to the librarians and staffs of the Central Library, University of California, San Diego and San Diego State University Library for their assistance with music materials.

May 15, 1980
San Diego, California

Harold Gleason
Warren Becker

CHAMBER MUSIC FROM HAYDN TO BARTÓK

OUTLINE I

INTRODUCTION

Music for Instrumental Ensembles before Haydn

I. **Instrumental Ensembles**

A. Instrumental ensembles have been known since the late thirteenth century, when polyphonic dances and motets for two or three instruments were first written down (*Codex Bamberg, c.* 1280).

B. During the fourteenth century instruments were widely used, alone and with voices.

C. In the fifteenth century, instrumental ensembles appeared in the *Glogauer Liederbuch* (*c.* 1480) and pieces were written by Johannes Ockeghem (*c.* 1420-1495), Henricus Isaac (*c.* 1450-1517), Paul Hofhaimer (1459-1537), Jacob Obrecht (1450-1505), Josquin des Prez (*c.* 1440-1521) and others.

D. The sixteenth-century instrumental ensembles were also strongly influenced by the vocal style.

   1. *Ricercari* for instrumental ensembles (or keyboard) were written by many composers, including Jacques Buus (1547), Adrian Willaert (1549), Andrea Gabrieli (1571).

   2. *Canzoni* for instrumental ensembles were written by Florentio Maschera (1584), Giovanni Gabrieli (1597) and others.

   3. Many dance pieces and a few fantasias were published in France and the Low Countries.

   4. Orlando di Lasso published in 1577 twelve pieces for two instruments. Eight *ricercari* are attributed to Giovanni Pierluigi da Palestrina.

   5. Fantasias in imitative style were written in England by William Byrd, Orlando Gibbons and Thomas Weelkes.

E. Seventeenth century

   1. At the beginning of the Baroque era the *basso continuo* (gamba and harpsichord) became a part of almost all ensemble music.

   2. *Canzoni*, sometimes called "sonatas," were written by Lodovico Grossi de Viadana (1602), Claudio Merulo (1608), Hans Leo Hassler (1601), Johann Hermann Schein (1609), Salomone Rossi (1608), Biagio Marini (1617), Girolamo Frescobaldi (1628).

   3. The *sonata da chiesa* and *sonata da camera* developed from the multisectional *canzone* about 1665.

     a. The *sonata da chiesa* (church sonata), so-called because it was performed in church, became a standard four-movement form (Adagio - Allegro - Adagio - Allegro).

       1) The third and fourth movements were often dance-like, however.

     b. The *sonata da camera* (chamber sonata), so-called because it was not intended for church or operatic use, included dance movements.

     c. Compositions in these two forms were written by Giovanni Batista Vitali (1667), Arcangelo Corelli (1681-1712), Henry Purcell (1683), Johann Rosenmüller (1667) and many others.

F. Eighteenth century

   1. The trio sonata (two violins and cello with *basso continuo*) developed about 1720 as a combination of elements found in both the *sonata da chiesa* and *sonata da camera*.

     a. It became the most important type of Baroque chamber music.

2. Trio sonatas were written by Francesco Geminiani, Giuseppi Torelli, Antonio Caldara, Nicola Porpora, Avaristo Felice dall'Abaco, Dietrich Buxtehude, George Frideric Handel and Johann Sebastian Bach (in the *Musical Offering*).
3. The string quartet (two violins, viola, bass or cello) appeared about 1745 with the addition of the viola and the discontinuing of the *basso continuo*. After about 1750 the cello was generally used instead of the bass viol.
4. The classical style began to develop about 1755.
    a. The rococo composers (c. 1725-1770), such as François Couperin (1668-1733) and others, played an important part in the development of form and expressiveness.
    b. Domenico Scarlatti, Giovanni Battista Pergolesi, Christoph Willibald Gluck, Giovanni Battista Sammartini and Giuseppe Sammartini made innovations in the development of the sonata-form. Pergolesi and Carl Philipp Emanuel Bach used the fast - slow - fast sequence.
    c. Johann Fasch and Georg Philipp Telemann sometimes omitted the *basso continuo* and included the viola.
5. The Viennese composers (*c*. 1740-1765) Josef Starzer, Georg Matthias Monn and Georg Christoph Wagenseil included the minuet, omitted the *basso continuo* and developed the sonata-form.
6. The Mannheim School (*c*. 1743-1800), founded by Johann Stamitz, made important contributions to the classical style in the matter of orchestral discipline and the use of crescendo and diminuendo, sudden fortes, homophonic writing, very fast allegros, "rocket" themes, tremolo, broken chords, and especially in the replacement of the *basso continuo* with written-out parts for instruments.
    a. Composers were Franz Xaver Richter, Ignaz Holzbauer, Carlo Giuseppe Toeschi and Christian Cannabich.
7. Contemporaries of Franz Joseph Haydn who were strongly influenced by the Mannheim composers include Johann Schobert (*c*. 1720-1767) and Johann Christian Bach (1735-1780). Schobert increased the importance of the piano in chamber music and J. C. Bach wrote quintets (1776) for flute, oboe, violin, viola and cello which are complete without the *basso continuo*, although it is indicated.
    a. Luigi Boccherini (1743-1805), a contemporary of Haydn, had considerable influence on the onward progress of chamber music, particularly the string quartet.

SELECTED BIBLIOGRAPHY

Books

1. Rowen, Ruth Halle. *Early Chamber Music*. New York: King's Crown Press, 1949. (reprint: New York: Da Capo Press, 1974)
2. Ulrich, Homer. *Chamber Music*, 2nd edition. New York: Columbia University Press, 1966.

Articles

1. Dent, Edward J. "The Earliest String Quartets." *Monthly Musical Record* 33 (1903), pp. 202-204.
2. Oberdoerffer, Fritz. "Changes of Instrumentation in the Chamber Music of the 18th Century." *JAMS* 4 (1951), pp. 65-66.
3. Pincherle, Marc. "On the Origins of the String Quartet." *MQ* 15 (1929), pp. 77-87.

OUTLINE II

FRANZ JOSEPH HAYDN (1732 - 1809)

I.   Life

1732   Born in Rohrau, Lower Austria, March 31. Left home at the age of five; received elementary instruction in Latin, singing, violin and harpsichord from a paternal cousin Johann Mathias Franck at Hainburg. Engaged by Georg Reutter (court composer and director of music) as chorister for St. Stephen's Cathedral in Vienna, and continued his education, mostly through his own efforts. Gave lessons, composed, practiced and played accompaniments. Studied by himself the sonatas and symphonies of Carl Philipp Emanuel Bach (1714-1788), Johann Joseph Fux's (1660-1741) *Gradus ad Parnassum* and Johann Mattheson's (1681-1764) *Der vollkommene Capellmeister.*

1755   Met Baron Karl Josef von Fürnberg of Weinzierl, near Vienna, through Pietro Metastasio the poet, and Nicola Porpora the singing teacher. Was employed by von Fürnberg as violinist for about a year and composed his first quartets. Became composer and director of music to Count Ferdinand Maximilian von Morzin at Lukavec, near Pilsen (1759). Married Maria Anna Keller in 1760.

1761   Entered the service of the powerful and wealthy Esterházy [Eszterházy] family (Prince Paul Anton, 1761-1762; Prince Nicolaus, 1762-1790) at Eisenstadt, Hungary. Here he provided two operatic performances and two formal concerts weekly. Publication of his music was begun by Artaria in Vienna (1769).

1790   Lived in Vienna after the death of Prince Nicolaus (1790). Made two visits to London (1791-1792; 1794-1795) under the concert management of Johann Salomon; wrote and conducted the twelve "Salomon" Symphonies; received the honorary Doctor of Music degree from Oxford University.

1798   Composed songs, quartets, two oratorios (*The Creation*, 1798; *The Seasons*, 1801) in his last years. Dictated to Johann Elssler, his copyist and secretary, a "catalogue of those compositions which I recall offhand having composed from my 18th to my 73rd year." Composed the Austrian national anthem, "The Emperor's Hymn" (1797).

1809   Died in Vienna on May 31 at the age of 77. Buried in the Hundsturm churchyard and later (1820) reinterred at Eisenstadt.

II.   Catalogue of Chamber Music

A.   String Instruments
   1.   Quartets
      a.   Eighty-four for 2 violins, viola, cello (1755-1809)
         1)   This number includes the "Interludes to the Seven Last Words, Op. 51," which Haydn arranged for string quartet, and the "Lost Heir," in E-flat major, Op. 1, No. 0, recently discovered. Included also is an incomplete work, Op. 103 in B-flat major.
      b.   One for lute, violin, viola, cello, in D major
   2.   Duos
      a.   Three for 2 violins
      b.   One for barytons, in G major (after 1762)
      c.   One for violin, cello, in D major (before 1783)
      d.   Six Sonatas for violin, viola (C major, A major, E-flat major, F major, D major,

              B-flat major) (after 1770)

    e. One for 2 lutes

3. Trios
    a. Eighteen for 2 violins, cello (harpsichord *ad lib.*) (E major, F major, D major, E-flat major, A major, B major, F major, C minor, E major, D major, C major, E-flat major, B-flat major, E major, G major, D major, D major, G major) (*c.* 1760).
    b. Twelve Divertimenti for 2 barytons, bass (cello) (after 1762)
    c. One hundred twenty-five for baryton, viola, cello (1762-1775)
       1) The baryton was a gamba-like instrument with six gut strings and twelve sympathetic strings. The sympathetic strings, usually metallic, were strung underneath the carved-out fingerboard. These could be plucked by the left thumb, while the gut strings over the fingerboard were bowed.
    d. One Cassation for lute, violin, cello, in C major
       1) Cassations designed for outdoor performance; especially adapted to music for weddings, festivals, birthdays, etc. Practically identical in form with Divertimenti and Serenades.
    e. One Divertimento for viola d'amore, violin, cello, in E-flat major (also in D major)

4. Quintets
    a. One for 2 violins, 2 cello, bass (flute *ad lib.*), in G major (1754)

5. Sextets
    a. "Echo" for 4 violins, 2 cellos (or piano, 2 violins, cello), to be performed in two separate rooms (before 1767)

B. String with Other Instruments
1. Eight Sonatas for violin, piano (harpsichord)
    a. G major (before 1790)
    b. D major (1773) from Piano Sonata No. 24 (Breitkopf & Härtel edition)
    c. E-flat major (1773) from Piano Sonata No. 25 (Breitkopf & Härtel edition)
    d. A major (1773) from Piano Sonata No. 26 (Breitkopf & Härtel edition)
    e. G major, Op. 70 (1794). The only composition composed originally in this form, others taken from piano sonatas, divertimenti or string quartets.
    f. C major (before 1767). A transcription of parts of a Divertimento for flute, oboe, 2 violins, cello, bass.
    g. F major (1799). A transcription of parts of String Quartet Op. 77, No. 2 (Minuet omitted).
    h. G major (1799). A transcription of parts of String Quartet Op. 77, No. 1 (Minuet omitted).

2. Trios
    a. Thirty-one for piano, violin, cello (*c.* 1770-1796)
       1) As numbered in the Breitkopf & Härtel edition: G major, F-sharp minor, C major, E major, E-flat major, D major, A major, C major, A major, E minor, E-flat major, E-flat major, B-flat major, G minor, E-flat major, G minor, E-flat major, C major, D minor, E-flat major, D major, B-flat major, F major, A-flat major, F major, C minor, F major, F major, G major, D major, G major.
    b. Three for piano, flute, bass
    c. Four for 2 flutes, cello (flute, violin, cello) (C major, G major, G major, G major) (1794)
    d. Two for flute, violin, bass (C major, G major, G major) (1794?)
    e. One Divertimento for horn, violin, cello, in E-flat major (1767)
    f. One for corno da caccia, violin, cello (1794?)
    g. One Sonata for harpsichord, flute, bass (1794)
    h. Three for 3 flutes
    i. One Trio Sonata (Divertimento) for piano, 2 violins, in B-flat major

3. Quartets

a. Six for flute, violin, viola, cello (1770)
b. One Divertimento for oboe, violin, viola da gamba, bass, in B-flat major (1767)
c. One for harpsichord, 2 violins, baryton, in F major (before 1762); published also as String Trio No. 25.
4. Sextets
    a. One for flute, oboe, bassoon, violin, cello, bass, in E-flat major (1782)
    b. One Divertimento for flute, oboe, 2 violins, cello, bass, in C major (Sonata No. 6 for violin, piano) (before 1767)
    c. One Cassation for flute, oboe, 2 violins, cello, bass, in G major (1768)
5. Octets
    a. One for 2 horns, 2 English horns, 2 violins, 2 basses (1760)
    b. One for 2 oboes, 2 clarinets, 2 bassoons, 2 horns, in F major (1760)
    c. Six Scherzandi for 2 horns, 2 oboes, flute, 2 violins, bass (F major, C major, D major, G major, E major, A major) (before 1757)
    d. One Divertimento for 2 English horns, 2 bassoons, 2 violins, 2 horns, in F major (1760)
    e. Six Divertimenti for flute, 2 horns, 2 violins, viola, cello, bass (G major, A major, G major, D major, G major, D major) (before 1781). All were previously baryton compositions, except No. 1.
    f. Six *Feld Partiten* for 2 oboes, 2 horns, 3 bassoons, serpent (or for 2 oboes, 2 clarinets, 2 horns, 2 bassoons) (*c.* 1780). *Feld Partita* in D-flat major, with the "Chorale St. Antonii," was used by Brahms in his Op. 56.
6. Nonets
    a. One for 2 oboes, 2 horns, 2 violins, viola, cello, bass (before 1757)
    b. One Cassation for 2 oboes, 2 horns, 2 violins, 2 cellos, bass, in G major
    c. Seven Notturni for 2 *lyra organizzata*, 2 clarinets, 2 horns, 2 violas, bass (C major, F major, G major, F major, C major, G major, D major) (1790)
        1) The *lyra organizzata* was a type of hurdy-gurdy, sometimes with small organ pipes. A typical hurdy-gurdy had a wheel handle and keyboard mounted on a small viol. Usually three or four bass strings which sounded in drone harmony continuously; two melody strings (tuned in unison) stopped by tangents operated by keys.

III. Chamber Music

A. Haydn was the first great master of the new instrumental style which culminated in the works of Beethoven. He refined and clarified the forms and achievements of his predecessors and effected the transition from the aesthetic system of Bach to that of the classicists in an orderly progression of works. He had original and inexhaustible melodic gifts and creative resources, and was a master of gaiety, humor, tenderness and passion.
    1. Problems of instrumentation, both in chamber music and the orchestra, many of which lay in the distribution of the continuo-function among all the instruments, were largely unresolved when Haydn began to compose. Among the problems were the special techniques of the various instruments and the contrasting and blending of tones of those instruments into the harmonic structure.
    2 A unique feature of Haydn's chamber music is his scoring of the same music for different instruments. His early chamber music often belongs more to orchestral literature than to chamber literature. In this category are the Divertimenti, Cassations, Nocturnes, Scherzi, and some smaller works. On the other hand, the violin and clavier sonatas as well as the clavier trios belong more to the field of piano literature.
B. Sonata-form (sonata-allegro; first-movement form)
    1. The form is usually used for the first, and sometimes for other movements of a quartet, symphony, concerto or sonata.

a.   The sonata-form has been in continual use since the time of Haydn, although in the twentieth century it has been subjected to many modifications.

2.   The sonata-form emerged from the cyclic binary form (A repeated - B - A repeated), with the use of two themes (often contrasting) in the first A section.

3.   Final development of the sonata-form (A - A - B - A or Exposition repeated - Development - Recapitulation).

a.   Exposition: Theme (group) I in the tonic. Theme (group) II in the dominant.

1)   If Theme I is in minor, Theme II will be in the relative major (Haydn and Mozart) or dominant minor.

2)   Bridge passages or transitions connect the themes.

3)   The closing theme at the end of Theme II is in the dominant.

a)   Later (Brahms) this theme often becomes Theme III.

b)   Repetition of the Exposition was usual until the time of Brahms.

b.   Development (fantasia). The function is to develop the material of the Exposition in various ways.

1)   Fragmentation of the themes.

2)   Rapid harmonic modulations.

3)   Use of contrapuntal devices.

4)   Occasional use of new themes.

c.   Recapitulation

1)   The material of the Exposition is restated more or less exactly. Bridge passages are usually modified.

2)   Theme (group) I is in the tonic.

3)   Theme (group) II is in the tonic.

d.   The Coda is usually short until the time of Beethoven.

C.   The String Quartet

1.   Haydn was vitally interested in the string quartet and made a special contribution to the form. He composed quartets for over fifty years, experimenting with contrapuntal forms, key relationships, and thematic development. Each quartet has a character of its own, and almost all show his steady musical progress.

2.   Major keys predominate; themes are usually diatonic (chromatic lines between 1785-1790); variations are usually of the *cantus firmus* type; there is considerable doubling in thirds and sixths; phrases are often of uneven length (five or seven measures).

3.   Chromatic lines appear in Op. 9, Nos. 1, 6; Op. 17, Nos. 2, 3, 6; Op. 20, Nos. 2, 4; Op. 33, Nos. 1, 3, 4; Op. 42. The principal use of chromatic lines is in Op. 50, 54, 55, 64; some use in the later quartets, Op. 71, No. 3; Op. 74, No. 1; Op. 77.

4.   Forms

a.   The sonata-form became the standard form for the first movement, and the rondo, sonata-rondo or sonata-form for the last movement.

b.   Variations are used for first movements in Op. 2, No. 6; Op. 3, No. 2; Op. 9, No. 5; Op. 17, No. 3; second movement in Op. 20, No. 4.

c.   Fugues are used for last movements in Op. 20, Nos. 2, 5, 6; Op. 50, No. 4.

d.   Minuets are used for both the second and fourth movements of Op. 1 and 2. Op. 1, No. 5 (a symphony) has only three movements (Fast - Slow - Fast). Op. 3, No. 4 has two movements (Fast - Slow, Fast, Slow, Fast).

1)   The Minuet is used for the second movements in Op. 3, Nos. 1, 2; Op. 9; Op. 17; Op. 20, Nos. 1, 3, 5; Op. 42; Op. 64, Nos. 1, 4; Op. 77, No. 2; Op. 103 (incomplete).

2)   The Minuet is used for the third movements in Op. 3, Nos. 3, 5, 6; Op. 20, Nos. 2, 4, 6; Op. 64, Nos. 1, 4.

e.   Scherzi are used for second movements in Op. 33, Nos. 1, 2, 3, 4; third movements in Nos. 5, 6. A Fantasia (Adagio) is the second movement in Op. 76, No. 6.

D.   Summary of Quartets

1. Op. 1 and 2 (1755), which include two minuets, were first known as divertimenti. Homophonic style, first violin prominent, two-part form predominates.
   a. Op. 3 (c. 1755-1765) established the four-movement form and a rudimentary sonata-form.
2. Op. 9 (c. 1769) shows for the first time, according to the composer, his real style.
3. Op. 17 (1771) marks a second advance in technique and expression.
4. Op. 20 (1772) reveals marked progress toward equality in the use of all four instruments, especially the cello, and the first use of fugue.
5. Op. 33 (1781) was "written in an entirely new manner" in which the use of thematic fragmentation and real thematic development are characteristic.
6. Op. 50, 51, 54, 55, 64 (1785-1790) were written during the years of Mozart's strongest influence upon Haydn. This influence is seen in many ways, including the use of chromatic lines, expansion of thematic material and expressive resourcefulness.
7. Op. 71, 74, 76, 77 (1791-1799) were concerned principally with considerations of expressiveness and the broadening of internal dimensions rather than in any basic alterations in design or precedure.

IV. String Quartets

A. Six Quartets. Op. 1: No. 1 in B-flat major ("La Chasse"). No. 2 in E-flat major, No. 3 in D major, No. 4 in G major, No. 5 in B-flat major (originally Haydn's first symphony), No. 6 in C major (c. 1755) (M 1, pp. 8, 11)
B. Six Quartets, Op. 2: No. 1 in A major, No. 2 in E major, No. 3 in E-flat major, No. 4 in F major, No. 5 in D major, No. 6 in B-flat major (1755)
   1. Op. 1 and 2 were written while Haydn was in the employ of Baron von Fürnberg (1755-1756). He was influenced primarily by works of Viennese pre-classicists Johann Adam Karl Georg Reutter, Georg Christoph Wagenseil and Georg Mathias Monn.
   2. Most of the quartets in Op. 1 and Op. 2 were known as "Divertimenti" for two violins, viola, and basso (cello or bass).
      a. Op. 1, No. 5 was originally a symphony for two oboes, two horns and strings.
      b. Op. 2, Nos. 3 and 5, were originally sextets with two horns (arranged by Haydn for string quartet).
   3. Op. 1 and Op. 2 have five movements each, which include two minuets (except Op. 1, No. 5). Usual order: Fast - Minuet - Slow - Minuet - Fast.
   4. The two-part forms used at first gradually show some evidences of a feeling for sonata-form.
      a. The second subject is in the dominant key, but often related to the first subject.
      b. The transitions between the second subject and the recapitulation became longer, suggesting a development section.
   5. Sequences, repetition, prominent first and second violins, doubling of the viola and cello (melodically or rhythmically), diatonic melodies, homophonic texture, irregular phrase lengths are a part of the style of the early quartets.
C. Six Quartets, Op. 3: No. 1 in E major, No. 2 in C major ("Fantasia con variazioni"), No. 3 in G minor (Minuet called "Bagpipe"), No. 4 in B-flat major, No. 5 in F major (with so-called "Serenade"), No. 6 in A major. (M 1, p. 15)
   1. Four movements become the standard form, with some exceptions.
      a. The Minuet is used second in Nos. 1 and 2, third in Nos. 3, 5, 6; different tempos are used for the first and final movements. The first movement of No. 2 is a theme and five variations.
      b. More ornamentation at cadence points; accompanying parts are given more independence; first and last movements are still very fast.
   2. Op. 3, No. 5 in F major. Presto - Andante cantabile - Menuetto - Scherzando.
      a. Four movements in the new order; Fast - Slow - Minuet - Fast. The first movement

shows the first real use of the sonata-form; the second theme is in direct contrast to the principal theme; the development section uses some unrelated keys; the transitions, codettas and closing themes are longer and more important.

   b.   First movement (Presto)

      1)   Exposition (meas. 1-90): first theme (meas. 1-16); codetta (meas. 17-23); transition (meas. 24-41); second theme (meas. 41-65); closing group (meas. 66-83); codetta (meas. 84-90).

      2)   Development (meas. 91-138): part of the first theme (meas. 91-98); melodic embellishment of the principal theme in D minor (meas. 99-106); development of a fragment of the theme from measure 24 in A major, D major, G major, G minor and F minor, using imitation (meas. 106-113).

      3)   Recapitulation (meas. 138-224): first theme slightly altered melodically (meas. 138-153); codetta altered harmonically (meas. 154-157); transition harmonically altered (meas. 158-175); second theme in the tonic, harmonically and melodically altered (meas. 176-199); closing group melodically altered (meas. 200-217); codetta as in measures 84-90 (meas. 218-224).

   c.   The famous "Serenade" has a typical song-like melody in the first violin with a pizzicato chordal accompaniment.

   d.   Last movement (Scherzando)

      1)   Sonata-form; Exposition: first theme (meas. 1-8); bridge (meas. 8); second theme (meas. 20); Development (meas. 45-61); Recapitulation (meas. 61).

V.   String Quartets, Op. 9, 17, 20 (1769-1772)

  A.   Six Quartets, Op. 9: No. 1 in C major, No. 2 in E-flat major, No. 3 in G major, No. 4 in D minor, No. 5 in B-flat major, No. 6 in A major (*c.* 1769)

    1.   Between Op. 3 and Op. 9 Haydn wrote forty symphonies. Haydn wished to discard the first eighteen quartets and begin with Op. 9, in which he felt his real style manifested itself. Op. 9 shows marked progress in quartet writing. The first violin part is still brilliant; themes are more imaginative, shorter, and better suited to development; longer development sections.

    2.   The first movement is a moderate Allegro (except No. 5, a theme and four variations); the second a Minuet; the third a slow movement; and the last movement retains its usual lively, humorous character.

    3.   Melodic lines are more elaborate, but still primarily diatonic; cadences are still sometimes ornamented; retardation of the leading-tone to the tonic is a common feature.

    4.   No. 2 in E-flat has an eight-measure recitative introduction to the slow movement. No. 4 in D minor uses dramatic pauses, syncopation, chromaticism and a scherzo-like finale. The first movement of No. 5 has a theme and four variations in a new form built on alternating themes. No. 6 makes some use of chromatic lines.

  B.   Six Quartets, Op. 17: No. 1 in E major, No. 2 in F major, No. 3 in E-flat major, No. 4 in C minor, No. 5 in G major, No. 6 in D major (1771)

    1.   New features appear; the style becomes richer, more profound and expressive in the slow movements.

      a.   The fast movements have more virtuoso-like first violin parts (double stops, arpeggios, crossing of strings and use of the highest register).

      b.   The material is more evenly divided among the instruments; more thematic material is given to the second violin, viola and cello; the viola and cello achieve more independence.

    2.   The Minuet is the second movement in all the quartets of Op. 17; the first movement of No. 3 is a Theme and Variations. The recitative idea is incorporated into the third movement (Adagio) of No. 5. Influence of Croatian folk songs is seen in No. 6.

  C.   Six Quartets, Op. 20: No. 1 in E-flat major, No. 2 in C major, No. 3 in G minor, No. 4

in D major, No. 5 in F minor, No. 6 in A major (*c.* 1772) (*M* 1, pp. 19, 23, 28, 35)

1. Called "Sun Quartets," from the symbol of the rising sun printed on an early edition. The names which are associated with the quartets were not given by Haydn. No one quartet is typical of the set; the individual differences between quartets are more marked than the similarities.

2. The form of the quartet, except for the Minuet, is finally established. The Minuet is used for the second movement in Nos. 1, 3, 5; the third movement in Nos. 2, 4, 6. In No. 4 it is in gypsy style (*alla zingarese*).

   a. The variation form is used for the second movement of No. 4.

   b. The final movments in Nos. 2, 5, 6 are four-voice fugues (the first use in the quartets), labelled two, three, or four subjects (*soggetti*), depending on how many counter-melodies accompany the principal subject throughout the fugue.

   c. The *style galant* is less in evidence; a new regard for tone color and melodic possibilities of the scale. True four-voice texture is gradually appearing as the cello becomes more important; fugal writing is the logical outcome.

3. No. 2 in C major: Moderato - Adagio - Menuetto - Allegro

   a. The first movement shows a fully developed sonata-form; begins with a cello solo (the first time the violin has not dominated); imitation is used between outer voices (meas. 48-60).

   b. The Adagio opens with a unison recitative suggestive of Beethoven, followed by a solo cadenza for violin.

   c. The Minuet uses "drone" figures.

   d. The fourth movement is a "*Fuga a IV Soggetti.*"

4. No. 5 in F minor: Allegro moderato - Menuetto - Adagio - Finale

   a. The first movement has first and second endings for the development and recapitulation; the movement concludes with an extended coda.

   b. The Adagio has a striking chain of dissonances (section marked "*per figuram retardationis*") caused by the first violin being slightly behind the change of chord.

   c. The Finale, "*Fuga a due Soggetti,*" is based on a theme similar to "And With His Stripes," from Handel's *Messiah*; stretto near the end of the fugue is separated by a pause on the dominant.

VI. String Quartets, Op. 33, 42 (1781-1783)

A. Six Quartets, Op. 33: No. 1 in B minor - D major, No. 2 in E-flat major ("The Joke"), No. 3 in C major ("The Bird"), No. 4 in B-flat major, No. 5 in G major, No. 6 in D major (1781). Dedicated to Grand Duke Paul of Russia. (*M* 1, pp. 42, 46, 52)

1. Haydn said these were "composed in a new and special manner" in which homophonic and polyphonic elements are satisfactorily combined. These quartets represent the first real thematic development; based on breaking up of phrases and contrapuntal development of the fragments. They are called "Russian" or, because of a picture on the title page, "*Jungfern*" Quartets; also known as "*Gli Scherzi,*" as each quartet has a movement marked "Scherzo" in place of the usual Minuet.

   a. The first time "Scherzo" appears in Haydn's chamber music; the term was not used after Op. 33, but the characteristics persisted in later Minuets.

2. Thematic material is still more evenly divided among the instruments; the initial melody sometimes is given to another instrument besides the first violin (No. 6, Andante, the second violin; No. 2, Largo, a duet for viola and cello).

   a. The melodies are diatonic, but with occasional chromatic lines (No. 1, Andante, sixth measure before the end; Nos. 3 and 4).

3. The major mode is used most, with modulations to closely related keys.

   a. "False starts," pizzicato, use of half-cadence and folk-like melodies give indications of Haydn's humor.

      b.   The Minuets are lighter and more Mozart-like, often with scherzo character.

      c.   There are fewer ornaments in the slow movements than in earlier periods, showing a change from "rococo" to "classic" style.

      d.   The Rondo form is used for the last movements, except in Nos. 1 and 5. The final movement of No. 6 consists of variations on two themes, one major and one minor (characteristic of Haydn).

    4.   No. 2 in E-flat major is called "The Joke" because of the humorous and unexpected ending of the Presto (finale); the theme of the Coda is a modified statment of the first theme; the cadence in measure 166 is like the end of the first section (meas. 8); the unexpected final cadence is like the opening of the movement measures 1-2.

      a.   This quartet is typical of this period, with emphasis on thematic and rhythmic development and better balance of parts.

      b.   The Development section of the first movement uses mostly motives from the first theme; modulations to G-flat major and D-flat major (meas. 46).

    5.   No. 3 in C major was called "The Bird" because of grace notes used and developed in the first and final movements, and the "bird-like" violin duet in the scherzando Trio. There is some influence of Croatian folk songs.

B.   Quartet Op. 42 in D minor (1768 or 1783 or 1785)

    1.   This quartet contains devices and elements seemingly suggesting both earlier and later styles, such as the dramatic development in the first movement, contrapuntal devices in the finale and pianissimo endings.

    2.   The first movement is slow; the second movement a Minuet; the third movement, marked "Adagio e cantabile," shows unique lyric writing with a long, singing melody; the Finale, marked "Presto," is written in imitative style; the second violin begins the theme.

VII.   String Quartets, Op. 50, 51, 54, 55, 64 (1785-1790)

A.   Six Quartets, Op. 50: No. 1 in B-flat major, No. 2 in C major, No. 3 in E-flat major, No. 4 in F-sharp minor, No. 5 in F major (with Adagio, "The Dream"), No. 6 in D major ("The Frog") (c. 1784) (M 1, p. 56)

    1.   Dedicated to Friedrich Wilhelm [Frederick William] II, King of Prussia, a capable cellist; emphasis is on cello parts; more difficult technically, richer, more lyrical and dramatic than in earlier quartets.

      a.   The first and second "themes" now often consist of several phrases, usually called "first group" and "second group."

      b.   Thematic development appears in the recapitulations as well as in the development sections.

      c.   A marked use of chromatic lines, which begins in these quartets, shows the influence of Mozart.

    2.   The Minuet is consistently used again, this time (and for most of the remaining quartets) as the third movement.

      a.   The Finales are all sonata-form except No. 4, which is a fugue (the last of the entirely fugal movements).

      b.   Fully developed and brilliant codas in place of the recapitulation (exact return of the first and second theme groups is no longer followed).

    3.   No. 4 in F-sharp minor has a change of mode between the first and second subjects of the first movement.

      a.   The Andante alternates between major and minor modes and combines rondo-like features with a theme and variations.

      b.   The key of six sharps is used for the first time (in the first movement and the Minuet).

      c.   The fourth movement is a fugue.

4. No. 5 in F major contains a slow movement known as "The Dream," from elaborate solo passages for the first violin.

    a. The third movement (Minuet and Trio) uses the same grace-note motif.

5. No. 6 in D major is called "The Frog" because of unique "croaking" sounds in the Finale, made by rapid alternation of the same note on two neighboring strings (bariolage).

    a. Unusual expansion of the Minuet Trio gives new treatment of material instead of the conventional re-use of a new theme.

B. Seven Quartets, Op. 51: No. 1 in D minor - B-flat major (Introduction and Largo), No. 2 in C minor - C major, No. 3 in E major, No. 4 in F minor, No. 5 in A major, No. 6 in G minor - G major, No. 7 in E-flat major - C minor (Largo with Presto "Earthquake")

1. Arranged by Haydn from the Good Friday music he composed for Cadiz Cathedral in 1785 under the title of "Seven Last Words of Christ."

    a. The original music was composed for orchestra, the form consisting of an Adagio introduction, seven slow movements in free sonata-form and a Finale.

    b. The vocal parts and a sacred text were added by Karl Friebert in 1792 and later revised by Haydn in collaboration with Gottfried van Swieten.

C. Three Quartets, Op. 54: No. 1 in G major, No. 2 in C major, No. 3 in E major (1788-1790). Dedicated to Johann Tost, a wealthy merchant. (M 1, pp. 61, 67)

1. The first movements are in sonata-form; the slow second movements are in the key of the subdominant or parallel mode; the Minuets are in the original key; the Presto Finales are also in the original key.

2. The writing is harmonic rather than contrapuntal, with thematic material well divided among the four instruments. The music in general shows an even greater melodic charm than in earlier works. Cadential dissonances are used more sparingly; some use of chromatic lines, but not in the main theme.

3. In No. 1 in G major, the second movement (Allegretto in C) has modulations to unusual keys (B-flat major, D-flat major, E-flat major, G-flat major).

4. No. 2 in C major has a large and symphonic first movement; dissonances built on a fourth (Minuet); crossing of parts (cello above violins and viola) in the Adagio introduction to the final Presto.

D. Three Quartets, Op. 55: No. 1 in A major, No. 2 in F minor ("The Razor"), No. 3 in B-flat major (1788-1790). Dedicated to Johann Tost. (M 1, pp. 74, 78)

1. From this point on, each quartet is a unique and individual masterpiece. The Minuet is still consistently used as the third movement; examples of chromaticism in each quartet in Op. 55.

2. No. 1 in A major has an Adagio in rondo form; employs extreme upper range of the violin in the Minuet; concludes with a Finale which begins as a rondo and ends as a double fugue.

    a. Some influence of Austrian and Hungarian folk melodies.

3. No. 2 in F minor is known as "The Razor" Quartet because of an exchange (a quartet for a good razor) bargained with a friend.

    a. The first movement is a set of variations in slow time, alternating major and minor.

E. Six Quartets, Op. 64: No. 1 in C major, No. 2 in B minor, No. 3 in B-flat major, No. 4 in G major, No. 5 in D major ("The Lark"), No. 6 in E-flat major (1790). Dedicated to Johann Tost. (M 1, pp. 82, 88, 93)

1. The forms are much the same as those already established; the slow movement follows the Minuet in Nos. 1 and 4; in the Finales a simple rondo form is replaced with well developed sonata-rondos.

2. New key relationships and keys appear in these and the following groups of quartets. Chromatic lines in Nos. 2, 4, 5, 6.

3. No. 5 in C major is called "The Lark" because of the upward-soaring, high melody in the first violin part. The Minuet has interesting canonic writing. The Finale is a

Gramley Library
Salem College
Winston-Salem, NC 27108

perpetuum mobile with a fugato at the beginning of the development section.

    4.   No. 6 in E-flat major. The last quartet of the Esterházy period, and a quartet of exceptional workmanship. More attention is given to the viola than before (development section of the first movement). The final Presto is built on a folk-like theme.

VIII.   **String Quartets, Op. 71, 74, 76, 77, 103 (unfinished) (1791-1803)**

  A.   These quartets show perfect balance between homophonic and polyphonic styles, combined with great freedom of form. Introductions, effective slow movements, and marked dynamic effects are characteristics. From Op. 71 on, the quartets are all on a symphonic scale.

  B.   Three Quartets, Op. 71: No. 1 in B-flat major, No. 2 in D major, No. 3 in E-flat major (1791-1793). Dedicated to Count Apponyi. (*M* 1, p. 99)

    1.   From Op. 71 on, the use of chromaticism is rare. The third movements are always in Minuet form. The slow movement of No. 3 is in rondo-variation form. The first movements have introductions (a feature of Haydn's symphony form), consisting of chords only in Nos. 1 and 3, and a four-measure Adagio in No. 2. Fugato is used at the beginning of the development section in the last movement of No. 1.

    2.   An interesting crossing of the cello and viola parts in No. 3 (development section of the first movement) produces second-inversion chords (meas. 129-132). The slow movement, in rondo-variation form, shows a new use of tone color. A little use of chromaticism.

  C.   Three Quartets, Op. 74: No. 1 in C major, No. 2 in F major, No. 3 in G minor ("The Rider") (1793-1794). Dedicated to Count Apponyi. (*M* 1, pp. 105, 113)

    1.   Tendencies toward romanticism and freedom in key relationships are characteristics of this group. Remote keys are used in the Trios of Minuets, a characteristic of quartets from Op. 74 on.

    2.   No. 1 in C major: the first movement opens with a two-chord introduction; fugato at the beginning of the development section. The first and final movements contain a development in the recapitulation. The Trio of the Minuet in C major goes to the remote key of A-flat major without modulation.

    3.   No. 2 in F major: the second movement (Andante grazioso) is composed of a theme and three florid variations; the second violin is prominent in the second variation. The Minuet shows a sharp key contrast (F major to D-flat major in the Trio). Influence of Croatian folk songs.

    4.   No. 3 is called "The Rider" from a galloping figure that introduces the first movement; fugato at the beginning of the development section. The second movement (Largo assai) in E major, has a short section in E minor. The brilliant Finale uses Hungarian and Austrian folk tunes.

  D.   Six Quartets, Op. 76: No. 1 in G major, No. 2 in D minor ("Quinten"), No. 3 in C major ("Emperor"), No. 4 in B-flat major ("Sunrise"), No. 5 in D major, No. 6 in E-flat major (with the "fantasia") (1797-1798). Dedicated to Count Erdödy.

    1.   These quartets reveal maturity of style and are direct, condensed, and intense in personal expression. The tempos are faster; the Minuets become more like Scherzi. Only two quartets and part of a third were composed after this opus. (*M* 1, p. 126)

    2.   An unusual feature is found in the Finales of Nos. 1 and 3 which begin in the parallel minor key. Fugal entries are found in No. 1 (first movement) and No. 6 (coda of first movement and "alternative" of Minuet).

    3.   No. 2 in D minor is called the "Quinten" because of descending fifths in the opening theme. "*Hexen* (Witches) Minuet" is a two-part canon between the violins in octaves and the viola and cello in octaves.

    4.   No. 3 in C major ("Emperor" or "Kaiser") includes the famous variations on "God Save Our Emperor" which later became the Austrian national anthem. Haydn set the

words to music in 1797 during the war between Austria and France. (*M* 1, p. 119)

    a.   The dotted-note rhythm (much used by Beethoven) of the first movement is found in the Minuet in reverse order. The four variations (second movement) use the theme without change, in the second violin, cello, viola, first violin. The Presto Finale in C minor is based on a triplet figure with many imitations and overlappings; slow sections serve to intensify the drive of the movement.

    b.   First movement (Allegro)

       1)   Exposition (meas. 1-44): the first theme is divided into three motives (meas. 1, 2, 3) used in various ways; a scale-line motive is in dotted-note rhythm combined with the first motive of the first theme (meas. 5-7); a bridge passage (meas. 8-12) over a tonic and dominant pedal closes on G (meas. 12); the first and third motives in imitation (meas. 13-17); transitory passages over a pedal point on D lead to a dominant seventh chord in G major (meas. 22), followed by a thematically important passage (meas. 23-25) leading to the second theme. The second theme (meas. 26-27) is related to the second motive of the first theme (meas. 2); a transitory passage (meas. 28) modulates to E-flat major (meas. 31); the first motive of the first theme is used in canonic imitation (meas. 33); the second theme is introduced in the dominant key (G major) and the exposition concludes in that key with first and second endings.

       2)   Development (meas. 45-78): material from the first theme, combined with the dotted-note rhythm (meas. 45-48); transition using the first two motives of the first theme (meas. 49-51); the second motive of the first theme (meas. 52-56); material from measures 23-25 (meas. 57-64) with a cadence in E major (meas. 65); the first theme and dotted-note rhythm with pedal point in open fifths (meas. 65-75); modulation to C major through C minor over a pedal point on E (meas. 75-78).

       3)   Recapitulation (meas. 79-121): repetition of material of the Exposition (meas. 79-87); a transitory passage in G major (meas. 90-94) leading to a dominant seventh in C major (meas. 94); codetta in C major (meas. 95-97); the second theme in the tonic (meas. 98).

       4)   Coda (meas. 105-121) uses a two-note motive from the first theme (meas. 105-107); modulating passage leads to the statement of the second theme in the tonic. The Development, Recapitulation and Coda are repeated.

    5.   No. 5 in D major includes the famous Largo in F-sharp minor. The first movement is in modified rondo form, the first phrase appearing more than twelve times.

    6.   No. 6 in E-flat opens with a set of variations on an allegretto theme. Adagio Fantasia of the second movement is in B major (first part has no key signature, accidentals are written for each note), with modulations to E major, G major, B-flat major, A-flat major and back to B major. The Minuet uses an ascending and descending E-flat major scale through all the parts.

E.   Two Quartets, Op. 77: No. 1 in G major, No. 2 in F major (1790). Dedicated to Prince Lobkowitz. (*M* 1, pp. 137, 145)

    1.   Transcribed by Haydn from his sonatas for flute and piano.

    2.   Experiments in the use of forms, thematic development and key relationships suggest the influence of Carl Philipp Emanuel Bach. There is some use of chromaticism in both quartets.

    3.   No. 1 in G major: the second theme (meas. 41) is omitted in the recapitulation of the first movement; symphonic treatment of ideas in the first movement. The second movement, Adagio, has an unusual key relationship (G major and E-flat major). The usual repeats in the Trio of the Minuet are omitted; the repetition is written out with several changes in the use of material.

    4.   No. 2 in F major: Minuet in F major, Trio in D-flat major, with coda (brief but formal) modulating back to F major by use of the first Minuet theme in the key of the

SALEM COLLEGE SCHOOL OF MUSIC

Trio. The Andante begins with two parts only; developed into a series of highly ornamented variations.

F.   Op. 103 (1803): Slow movement and Minuet only.

    1.   Op. 103 is usually referred to as in the key of B-flat, but from the key of the Minuet it should be called D minor, since Haydn wrote his minuets in the tonic key of the quartet. The keys in the main sections of the first movement (Andante grazioso) are B-flat major, G-flat major to D-flat major, C-sharp minor (same as D-flat minor) and B-flat major.

    2.   In 1806 despairing of finishing the quartet, Haydn added at the conclusion of the Minuet the melody with these words from a vocal quartet, *Der Greis* (Old Age): "Gone is all my strength, old and weak am I."

SELECTED BIBLIOGRAPHY

Books

1.   Barret-Ayres, Reginald. *Joseph Haydn and the String Quartet*. New York: Schirmer Books, 1974.
2.   Brenet, Michel. *Haydn*, tr. C. Leonard Leese. London: Oxford University Press, 1926.
3.   Fox, Douglas Gerard Arthur. *Haydn*. London: Oxford University Press, 1929.
4.   Geiringer, Karl. *Haydn, A Creative Life in Music*, 2nd rev. ed. London: Allen & Unwin, 1964.
5.   ————Berkeley: University of California Press, 1968. (paperback)
6.   Griesinger, Georg August, and Albert Christoph Dies. *Joseph Haydn: Eighteenth-Century Gentleman and Genius*, tr. Vernon Gotwals. Madison: University of Wisconsin Press, 1963.
7.   ————*Haydn: Two Contemporary Portraits*. Madison: University of Wisconsin Press, 1968. (reprint of No. 6 above) (Contains *Biographical Notes Concerning Joseph Haydn*. Leipzig: Breitkopf & Härtel, 1810; and *Biographical Accounts of Joseph Haydn*. Vienna: Camesina Bookshop, 1810)
8.   Hadden, J. Cuthbert. *Haydn*. New York: E. P. Dutton, 1934.
9.   Hadow, William Henry. *A Croatian Composer; notes toward the study of Joseph Haydn*. London: Seeley and Co., 1897.
10. Hoboken, Anthony van. *Joseph Haydn Thematisch-bibliographisches Werkverzeichnis*. Mainz: B. Schott's Söhne, 1957.
11. Hughes, Rosemary. *Haydn*. London: J. M. Dent, 1956; New York: Farrar, Straus and Cudahy, 1956. (Chamber Music: pp. 150-169).
12. Jacob, Heinrich Eduard. *Joseph Haydn, His Art, Times, and Glory*, tr. Richard and Clara Winston. New York: Holt, Rinehart and Winston, 1950.
13. Landon, H. C. Robbins. *Haydn: Chronicle and Works*, 4 volumes. Bloomington: Indiana University Press, 1977.
14. ————*The Piano Trios of Joseph Haydn*. Vienna: Verlag Doblinger, 1970.
15. Pohl, Karl Ferdinand. *Joseph Haydn*, 3 volumes (Volume III by Hugo Botstiber). Leipzig: Breitkopf & Härtel, 1875-1927.
16. ————*Mozart and Haydn in London*. Vienna: C. Gerolds Sohn, 1867.
17. Raynor, Henry B. *Joseph Haydn; His Life and Work*. London: Boosey & Hawkes, 1961.
18. Rosen, Charles. *The Classical Style: Haydn, Mozart, Beethoven*. New York: Viking Press, 1971. (Haydn: String Quartets, pp. 111-142; Piano Trios, pp. 351-365)
19. Tovey, Donald F. *Essays in Musical Analysis: Chamber Music*. London: Oxford University Press, 1956.
20. Townsend, Pauline D. *Joseph Haydn*. London: S. Low and Co., 1894.

Articles

1. Adler, Guido. "Haydn and the Viennese Classical School," tr. Oliver Strunk. *MQ* 18 (1932), pp. 191-207.
2. Bell, A. Craig. "An Introduction to Haydn's Piano Trios." *MR* 16 (1955), pp. 191-197.
3. Botstiber, Hugo. "Haydn and Luigia Polzelli." *MQ* 18 (1932), pp. 208-215.
4. Clarke, Rebecca. "The History of the Viola in Quartet Writing." *ML* 4 (1923), pp. 6-17.
5. Fry, J. "Haydn's String Quartets Op. 20." *MT* 85 (1944), p. 140.
6. Keller, Hans. "The Interpretation of the Haydn Quartets." *Score* 24 (Nov 1958), pp. 14-35.
7. –––––––"The String Quartet and Its Relatives [String Quartets, Op. 20, Nos. 1-4]." *MR* 26 (1965), pp. 340-344; 27 (1966), pp. 59-62; 228-232; 232-235.
8. –––––––"Today's Tomorrow [String Quartet, Op. 9, No. 4]." *MR* 26 (1965), pp. 247-251.
9. Landon, H. C. Robbins. "Doubtful and Spurius Quartets and Quintets Attributed to Haydn." *MR* 18 (1957), pp. 213-221.
10. Lowinsky, Edward E. "On Mozart's Rhythm [Comparison of Haydn's Phrase Structure with Mozart's]." *MQ* 42 (1956), pp. 162-186.
11. Moe, Orin. "Texture in Haydn's Early Quartets." *MR* 35 (1974), pp. 4-22.
12. Muller, Joseph. "Haydn Portraits." *MQ* 18 (1932), pp. 282-298.
13. Randall, J. K. "Haydn: String Quartet in D major, Op. 76, No. 5." *MR* 21 (1960), pp. 94-105.
14. Salzer, Felix. "Haydn's Fantasia from the String Quartet, Op. 76, No. 6." *Music Forum* 4 (1976), pp. 161-194.
15. Saslav, Isidor. "Latest Discoveries in the Haydn Quartets." *Am Mus Teacher* 25, No. 1 (1975), pp. 18-20.
16. Schmid, Ernst Fritz. "Mozart and Haydn [Their Influence on Each Other]," tr. Ernest Sanders. *MQ* 42 (1956), pp. 145-161.
17. Scott, Marion M. "Haydn's Chamber Music." *MT* 73 (1932), p. 212.
18. –––––––"Haydn's '83': A Study of the Complete Editions." *ML* 11 (1930), p. 207.
19. –––––––"Haydn in England." *MQ* 18 (1932), pp. 260-273.
20. Silbert, Doris. "Ambiguity in the String Quartets of Joseph Haydn." *MQ* 36 (1950), pp. 562-573.
21. Smith, Carleton Sprague. "Haydn's Chamber Music and the Flute." *MQ* 19 (1933), pp. 341-350; 434-455.
22. Strunk, Oliver. "Haydn's Divertimenti for Baryton, Viola, and Bass." *MQ* 18 (1932), pp. 218-251.
23. Tyson, Alan. "Haydn and Two Stolen Trios." *MR* 22 (1961), pp. 21-27.
24. Webster, James C. "The Bass Part in Haydn's Early String Quartets." *MQ* 63 (1977), pp. 390-424.
25. –––––––"The Chronology of Haydn's String Quartets." *MQ* 61 (1975), pp. 17-46.
26. –––––––"Towards a History of Viennese Chamber Music in the Early Classical Period." *JAMS* 27 (1974), pp. 212-247.
27. –––––––"Violoncello and Double Bass in the Chamber Music of Haydn and His Viennese Contemporaries, 1750-1780." *JAMS* 29 (1977), pp. 413-438.
28. Willfort, E. H. "Haydn's Compositions for Mechanical Instruments." *MT* 73 (1932), p. 510.
29. Wollenberg, Susan. "Haydn's Baryton Trios and the 'Gradus' [Fux]." *ML* 54 (1973), pp. 170-178.

Music

Study (Miniature) Score

1. *The Chamber Music of Haydn and Schubert*, ed. Albert E. Wier. Melville, NY: Belwin-Mills, 1973.
2. *83 String Quartets*, 3 vols. (*EE*)
   a. Vol. 1: Op. 1, 2, 3, 9, 17 (Nos. 1-30)
   b. Vol. 2: Op. 20, 33, 42, 50, 51, 54 (Nos. 31-59)
   c. Vol. 3: Op. 55, 64, 71, 74, 76, 77, 103 (Nos. 60-83)
3. *30 Celebrated String Quartets*, 3 vols. (*KSS*)
4. *Eleven Late String Quartets: Opp. 74, 76 and 77*, ed. Wilhelm Altmann. New York: Dover Publications. (reprint: Eulenberg miniature)
5. *31 Piano Trios* (*Lea* 121, 122, 123, 124)

Playing Parts and Scores

6. *Streichquartette* (complete), ed. Reginald Barrett-Ayres and H. C. Robbins Landon. Vienna: Verlag Doblinger, 1968-1977. (parts and pocket scores)
7. *Streichquartette*, 5 vols. to date. Munich: G. Henle Verlag, 1969.
8. *Sämtliche 83 Quartette für zwei Violinen, Viola, und Violoncello*, 4 vols. New York: C. F. Peters. (*PE* 15a, 15b, 289a, 289b)
9. *Klaviertrios* (complete), ed. H. C. Robbins Landon. Vienna: Doblinger Verlag, 1974.
10. *Trios für Klavier, Violine und Violoncello*, 2 vols., ed. Wolfgang Stockmeier. Munich: G. Henle Verlag, 1976.
11. *Trios für Pianoforte, Violine und Violoncello*, 3 vols. New York: C. F. Peters. (*PE* 192a, 192b, 192c)
12. *Three Trios*, Op. 32 (violin, viola, cello). New York: International Music Company.
13. *Three Trios*, Op. 53 (violin, viola, cello). New York: International Music Company.
14. *String Trios*, Op. 21, 32 (violin, viola, cello). London: Edition Peters.
15. *Trios für Klavier, Flöte und Violoncello* (complete). Munich: G. Henle Verlag, 1976.
16. *Sextet* No. 14 in E-flat (violin, viola, cello, oboe horn, bassoon), ed. K. Janetsky. London: Musica Rara, 1957; New York: Mercury, 1957.
17. (*CE*) *Joseph Haydn Werke*, ed. Georg Feder, Joseph Haydn Institute, Cologne. Munich: G. Henle Verlag, 1958- (in progress).
    a. String Quartets: Series 12, vol. 1 (Op. 1, 2, 3); vol. 2 (Op. 9, 17); vol. 3 (Op. 20, 33).

OUTLINE III

WOLFGANG AMADEUS MOZART (1756 - 1791)

I. Life

1756   Born in Salzburg, Austria, January 27.

1760   Began clavier lessons with his father; first pieces composed (1761).

1762   Visited Munich, Vienna (gave concert at Linz) and Pressburg with his father, Leopold, and his sister, Marianne.

1763   Salzburg; Mozarts (Wolfgang, father and sister) began a concert tour in June, going to Belgium, Holland, France and Switzerland. Entertained at Versailles by Louis XV; played at the court in London; met Johann Christian Bach. Returned to Salzburg (1766).

1769   Performed in the prominent cities of Italy; studied with Padre Giambattiste Martini in Milan; began to compose quartets.

1771   After only five months in Salzburg, again father and son went to Italy.

1772   Returned to Salzburg; active period of composition; went again to Milan.

1773   Milan; Salzburg; Vienna. Quartets K. 168-173 written in Viennese style. He composed no more quartets until 1782. Visited Munich.

1776   Salzburg; difficulties with Archbishop Heironymous.

1777   Mannheim; met Fridolin Weber family; daughter Constanze later to become his wife.

1778   Journeyed to Mannheim with his mother; continued on to Paris; mother died in Paris; again met J. Christian Bach. Returned to Salzburg (1779) by way of Strasbourg, Mannheim and Munich.

1781   Famous contest with Muzio Clementi at Court of Prince-Archbishop of Salzburg. In Vienna, first meeting with Franz Joseph Haydn, a friend until his death.

1782   Began composition of the "Haydn" quartets. Married Constanze Weber, August 4, and made Vienna their home. From this time until his death, Mozart was without a regular position and his life was one of disappointment, discouragement and poverty.

1784   Vienna; met Giuseppe Sarti and Giovanni Paisiello; Salzburg, Linz.

1787   Prague (first performance of *Don Giovanni*); Vienna (met Beethoven); father died.

1789   Visited Dresden, Leipzig, Berlin, with Prince Karl Lichnowsky. Went on to Potsdam where he was presented to the king, Frederick William II, a cellist.

1790   Played his "Coronation" Piano Concerto in D major at Frankfurt, for the coronation of Emperor Leopold. On his return to Vienna, visited Mainz, Mannheim, Munich.

1791   Vienna; received a mysterious commission for a *Requiem*. The *Requiem* was unfinished at his death on December 5; he was buried in a pauper's grave.

II. Catalogue of Chamber Music

A. String instruments
  1. Quartets
    a. Twenty-six for 2 violins, viola, cello
  2. Quintets
    a. Five for 2 violins, 2 violas, cello
  3. Trios
    a. One for violin, viola, cello
    b. One for 2 violins, bass, continuo

SALEM COLLEGE SCHOOL OF MUSIC

    4.   Duos
      a.   Two for violin, viola

B.   Piano and other instruments
    1.   Forty-two sonatas for violin, piano
    2.   Trios
      a.   Seven for piano, violin, cello
      b.   One for piano, clarinet, viola
    3.   Quartets
      a.   Two for piano, violin, viola, cello
    4.   Quintet
      a.   Piano, oboe, clarinet, horn, bassoon

C.   String and wind instruments
    1.   Five Divertimenti
    2.   Three quartets
      a.   Two for flute, violin, viola, cello
      b.   One for oboe, violin, viola, cello
    3.   Two quintets
      a.   One for 2 violins, viola, cello, clarinet
      b.   One for violin, 2 violas, cello, horn
    4.   One duet for bassoon, cello

D.   Wind instruments
    1.   Twelve duets for 2 horns
    2.   Five Divertimenti for 2 clarinets, bassoon
    3.   Miscellaneous works with basset horn

III. Chamber Music

A.   Within a short space of thirty-six years, Mozart proved himself the most comprehensive musical genius who ever lived, bringing to everything he touched the perfection of a master. The best-known qualities of his music are brightness, gaiety and serenity. There is, however, a deeper, more tragic note, an underlying tenderness and melancholy.

    1.   One of the least nationalistic of the great composers, Mozart, in spirit and style, was more Italian than German. Working instinctively, he brought unlimited resourcefulness to each form of creative music.

B.   Mozart received his early training from his father, an excellent musician and teacher, and the author of a famous violin method.

    1.   In his visits to Paris and London, he became acquainted with the music of Johann Schobert and Johann Christian Bach.
    2.   He knew the *Gradus ad Parnassum* of Johann Joseph Fux as early as 1766 and became thoroughly familiar with the contrapuntal style of German and Austrian composers.
    3.   He was strongly influenced by the light, melodious and spontaneous rococo style found in the works of Giovanni Sammartini, Johann Christian Bach and others.

C.   Mozart composed chamber music throughout his life. His first violin sonata was written at the age of seven, his last quintet in the year of his death.

    1.   The style and form of chamber music was not clearly defined when he began to compose. By the time of his death, however, chamber and symphonic styles had become completely separated, and sonata-form and over-all forms were established, though both were still capable of expansion.
    2.   Chamber works form roughly about one-fifth of Mozart's total compositions. His progress as a composer may be most clearly seen in the violin sonatas, written from his earliest to most mature period.

D.   The 26 quartets may be divided into two large groups, which may in turn be subdivided.

    1.   K. 80; K. 136-138; K. 155-160; K. 168-173 (1770-1773)

2. The six "Haydn," the "Hoffmeister," and the three "Prussian" quartets (1782-1790).

E. K., used to identify Mozart's compositions, is the abbreviation for Ludwig von Köchel, who catalogued the Mozart works in his *Chronologisch-thematisches Verzeichnis sämtlicher Tonwerke W. A. Mozarts*, Leipzig, 1862. It has been revised several times since.

IV. Early String Quartets (1770-1773)

A. The early string quartets show the influence of other composers on his style, foreshadow devices that are associated with his mature works and show the growth of the formal aspects of his style.

1. K. 80 in G major (1770)

   a. Not a true quartet. Originally only three movements; the Rondo was added in 1773. Written during his first visit to Italy. The influence of Giovanni Battista Sammartini and the north Italian trio sonata is seen in the large number of short melodies and the arrangement of tempos in the movements (Adagio, Allegro, Minuet with Trio), the unity of key and the general homophonic style.

   b. The first violin has most of the melodic material; the second violin has many passages in sixths, thirds and tenths with the first violin; the viola and cello have accompaniment figures.

2. Three quartets: K. 136 in D major; K. 137 in B-flat major; K. 138 in F major (1772)

   a. Written in Salzburg. They were designated "divertimenti" on the original manuscript (probably not by Mozart), but are unlike divertimenti in having only three movements and no minuets. Possibly intended to be used either as quartets, or with the addition of horn and oboe parts as symphonies.

   b. The principal interest lies in the two violin parts; the two lower parts consist mostly of repeated quarter notes marking the harmony. The opening themes are often built on tonic chord figures. Fast movements have sudden changes of dynamics; final cadences often end with repeated chords.

   c. The Developments are sectional; one theme is used before going to the next. The material is not always literal; may be only a rhythmic recalling of material used in the Exposition or new material.

   d. Sonata-forms are mostly three-part, but with short Developments. K. 138 introduces a new subject in the Development. Andante, K. 138, is in two-part form; the first theme appears immediately after the double bar in the key of the dominant, followed by the second theme in the tonic key.

   e. K. 137 has the same key throughout the three movements; K. 136 and K. 138 each have a middle movement in a contrasting key.

   f. K. 137 shows Mozart's skill in handling the return of the second theme in the Recapitulation of the first movement.

3. Six quartets: K. 155 in D major; K. 156 in G major; K. 157 in C major; K. 158 in F major; K. 159 in B-flat major; K. 160 in E-flat major (1772-1773)

   a. Keys in a circle of fourths. All have three movements. The first movement is fast, second slow, except K. 159 which reverses the order.

   b. In *concertante* style, first and second violins against viola and cello, or solo violin against second violin and viola with cello as *continuo*. First and second violins have many passages in thirds, sixths, octaves and tenths.

   c. The dynamics are apt to be strongly and suddenly contrasted (Mannheim influence). The Developments are sectional.

   d. More interest in lower voices; the first theme announced by the second violin (K. 159); the cello uses imitation (K. 159).

   e. Greater contrast between first and second themes than before.

4. Six quartets: K. 168 in F major; K. 169 in A major; K. 170 in C major; K. 171 in E-flat major; K. 172 in B-flat major; K. 173 in D minor (1773)

a.   In Viennese style. Written after Mozart knew Haydn's Op. 17 and Op. 20, and are strongly influenced by these. New features include: four-movement form; contrapuntal texture and resultant independence and importance of the three lower instruments; thematic instead of sectional developments; a new economy of material (a transitional passage, for instance, may grow out of a figure in the first theme).

b.   Other indications of Haydn's influences are: use of slow introduction (K. 171); fugue for the last movement (K. 168; K 173); typical Haydn nine-measure period divided into 3 - 2 - 2 - 2 measure phrases (K. 168); first movement (K. 170) an Andante with variations.

c.   Foreshadowings of Mozart's later style are seen in the chromaticism in the last part of some of the main themes (K. 168, the Minuet of K. 170), and in the use of a third relationship between the main theme and the transition of the Andante in K. 169.

V.   Late Quartets   (1782-1790)

A.   Mozart wrote no string quartets between 1773 and 1782. In the meantime, Haydn brought out six quartets, Op. 33 (1781). Mozart studied them and was profoundly impressed. In these nine years his harmonic style had matured; he had written, among other things, twelve symphonies and one important opera (*Idomeneo*).

B.   His late quartets have all of the characteristics of his mature style: use of short chromatic lines, harmonic freedom, perfection of form, closely knit contrapuntal texture. Some characteristics of earlier works are still present: doubling in tenths, thirds and sixths; preference for the subdominant key for the slow movement. Codas are often longer and more developed.

C.   Six "Haydn" Quartets: K. 387 in G major, K. 421 in D minor, K 428 in E-flat major, K. 458 in B-flat major, K. 464 in A major, K. 465 in C major (1782-1785)

1.   These six quartets and the last four are also known as the "Ten Celebrated Quartets."

2.   Mozart's dedication begins: "To my dear friend Haydn! A father who has concluded to send his children into the world at large, thought best to entrust them to the protection and guidance of a famous man who fortunately happened to be his best friend as well."

3.   K. 387 in G major   (*M* 1, p. 9)

a.   Allegro vivace assai in G major. Sonata-form.

1)   Exposition (meas. 1-55); principal section (meas. 1-24); the first subject alternates diatonic and chromatic motives (meas. 1-4); the viola introduces a motive (meas. 5) which is answered by the second and first violin; subsidiary section (meas. 25-38); second theme (meas. 25-26) in the dominant; the viola doubles the violin at tenths (meas. 31-34); closing section (meas. 39-55).

2)   Development (meas. 56-107); a motive of the first theme in D major in the first violin (meas. 56), in E minor in the second violin, (meas. 61), in C major in the viola (meas. 68); imitation of a scale-like motive in violins (meas. 70-79); dotted note figure at the end of the Exposition (meas. 54-55) repeated in E minor (meas. 88-89) and in the same key of D major (meas. 99-100); an imitative trill passage leads to a dominant seventh chord and the Recapitulation.

3)   Recapitulation (meas. 108-170); varied treatment of material of the Exposition; second theme in the tonic as usual.

b.   Menuetto: Allegro in G major - G minor. Modified sonata-form.

1)   The first subject is diatonic (meas. 1-2), followed by chromatic scale lines with alternating *p* - *f* which produces a two-beat effect; the second subject is in the dominant (meas. 21). The second section begins with a short development and a recapitulation follows (meas. 63) with a return of the second subject in the tonic (meas. 74). The Trio in G minor uses an ascending arpeggio trill motive; some imitative writing in the second section.

c. Andante cantabile in C major. Modified sonata-form.
1) The Exposition (meas. 1-51) is divided into a principal section (meas. 1-30), subsidiary section (meas. 30-46); the closing section (meas. 46-48) leads to a short transitory passage (meas. 48-51) which replaces the Development.
2) The Recapitulation (meas. 51-106) varies the Exposition with special emphasis on the repeated-note motive; the second theme (meas. 87-88) is in the tonic.
d. Molto allegro in G major. Free sonata-form with fugal sections.
1) Exposition (meas. 1-125); the principal section (meas. 1-51) begins with a fugal exposition (meas. 1-17); the subject recalls the fugue of the "Jupiter" Symphony; free responsive section (meas. 17-51); responsive section concludes with a chromatic passage with a pedal point on A varied at the end (meas. 39-51). Subsidiary section (meas 51-107); fugal exposition of the second subject (meas. 51-68) which is combined with the first fugue subject (meas. 69-91); a solo section corresponding to the first free section (meas. 92-106); closing section (meas. 107-119); transitory passage leading, with a chromatic motive (meas. 120-124), to the Development.
2) The Development (meas. 125-174) opens with the chromatic motive; the first fugue subject reappears in the first violin and cello, passing through remote keys (meas. 143-159).
3) The Recapitulation (meas. 175-266) has no clearly defined starting point (Beethoven); begins with free responsive section in sub-dominant; the second subject in the tonic combined with the first fugue subject (meas. 209-234); solo section in the tonic (meas. 235-242); closing section and transitory passage lead to the Coda.
4) The Coda (meas. 266-298) begins with the chromatic motive of the Development; stretto of the first fugue subject in the first violin, viola, cello (meas. 282-287).
4. K. 421 in D minor   (*M* 1, p. 18)
a. Allegro in D minor. Sonata-form.
1) Exposition (meas. 1-41); principal section and modulation (meas. 1-24); subsidiary section (meas. 25-35); second theme in the relative major (F major) (meas. 25-26); closing section (meas. 35-41); codetta fugue in the first violin (meas. 39) used in the Development.
2) The Development (meas. 42-69) begins suddenly in E-flat major with a two-measure motive of the first theme; dissonant imitation (meas. 53-58); use of codetta figure at the end of the Exposition (meas. 59-70).
3) The Recapitulation (meas. 70-112) has a slight alteration of material; second theme in D minor, slightly varied (meas. 94-95).
4) The Coda (meas. 112-117) is short; uses the codetta motive.
b. Andante in F major. Ternary form with Coda.
1) Part I (meas. 1-26), principal section (meas. 1-8), middle section (meas. 9-14), expanded recapitulation of the principal section (meas. 15-26). Part II (meas. 26-51) is a free variation of the theme. Part III is a recapitulation of Part I (meas. 52-77). Coda (meas. 77-86).
c. Menuetto: Allegretto in D minor - D major
1) Serious style. The contrasting Trio uses an unusual sixteenth- and dotted-eighth-note rhythm; a rare use of pizzicato (only important use in any of Mozart's string quartets).
d. Allegro ma non troppo in D minor
1) Theme and four variations in "Siciliano" rhythm. Variation No. 4 in D major. The Coda (meas. 113-142) returns to the theme with some alterations.
5. K. 428 in E-flat major (*M* 1, p. 24)
a. The first movement, Allegro ma non troppo, begins with the theme in unison; the second theme (meas. 40) finally establishes the dominant (B-flat major). The Devel-

opment uses the first theme in canon and the first motive of the second theme.

b. The Andante in A-flat major is in sonata-form with a short development section.

c. The Trio (B-flat major) of the Menuetto uses pedal points on C, B-flat, G. F and B-flat.

d. The Finale, Allegro vivace in E-flat major, is in the style of Haydn; in Rondo form, it is based largely on material from measures 1-8 and 60-67.

6. K. 458 in B-flat major (*M* 1, p. 32)

a. The horn call at the opening gave the name of "The Hunt" quartet; second theme (meas. 54). The development begins with a new theme (meas. 91) in F major, ending in F minor (meas. 106). The Recapitulation (meas. 138-231) is followed by an unusually long Coda (meas. 232-279) which uses the hunting theme in imitative passages.

b. The second movement is a Minuet and Trio in B-flat major.

c. An Adagio (E-flat major) movement used for the only time in the "Haydn" quartets. Sonata-form; principal section (meas. 1-14); contrasting second theme (meas. 15).

d. The Finale is in sonata-form (possibly rondo) with three subjects: 1) measuse 1-4; 2) measure 48-50; 3) measure 82-85. Closing section of Exposition (meas. 81-121) and Coda (meas. 122-133). The Development (meas. 134-199) is based on the first subject. The Recapitulation (meas. 200-319) uses all three subjects in the tonic key of B-flat. Coda (meas. 320-335).

7. K. 464 in A major (*M* 1, p. 40)

a. The principal theme is in a new style; based on two motives; use of chromaticism; unison passage based on principal theme (meas. 9-12); key of the dominant reached through C major and an augmented sixth on C (meas. 32). The second subject begins in measure 37. The Development (meas. 88-161) is based largely on the principal theme and the unison theme of measures 9-12. Recapitulation (meas. 162-270).

b. The Minuet (A major - E major) is based on two melodic sequences which are combined (meas. 9-12), and used in canonic imitation and inversion. The Trio is in E major.

c. The Andante movement (D major) is a theme (divided into two parts, each repeated) with six variations and a Coda variation. Variation VI is built over a strongly rhythmic dominant pedal which is also used in the Coda.

d. The Finale (A major) opens with a chromatic motive and makes frequent use of sequences. In sonata-form with the second subject almost identical with the first subject (meas. 40-45) which gives the effect of only one main theme. The Exposition (meas. 82-144) is based mostly on the second subject; interrupted by a chorale-like section (meas. 114) which uses the chromatic first motive in augmentation (meas. 118-119). The Recapitulation begins in measure 145; the second subject returns in the tonic (meas. 185). Coda (meas. 230-262).

8. K. 465 in C major (*M* 1, p. 49)

a. This contains the famous "dissonant" chromatic introduction; parts written in "linear" style. The slow Introduction to the first movement is unique; it is the only one in the series. Unity in style is achieved by melodic chromaticism and the device of melodic reiteration of tones, both being characteristics of all movements.

b. Unusual features are: a beginning vague in harmonic intent; cross relations (meas. 2, 6); change of mode in the Minuet (C major to C minor).

c. In the final movement are found third relationships (meas. 88-89; 291-292), canonic writing between the first violin and cello (D-flat major) with imitation at a distance of three octaves (meas. 308-318).

D. K. 499 in D major (1786) Dedicated to Franz Anton Hoffmeister. (*M* 1, p. 58)

1. During 1786 Mozart was writing *The Marriage of Figaro* and composed only one string quartet. The quartet shows freedom within the sonata-form (development passages at

unexpected places in both first and last movements); freedom in modulation (the development of the first movement has a series of modulations from A minor to E-flat major and then to D major by means of the enharmonic nature of the dominant seventh of E-flat major and the German sixth of D major).

E. Three Prussian Quartets: K. 575 in D major; K. 589 in B-flat major; K. 590 in F major (1789-1790) (*M* 1, pp. 68, 76, 83)

1. Commissioned by King Frederick William II of Prussia, an amateur cellist. As a result the cello is prominent, sometimes solo (Minuet, K. 575); frequently in high range, even reaching e".

VI. Five String Quintets

A. Mozart first became acquainted with the quintet in Italy, from the works of Giovanni Battista Sammartini. Later in Salzburg, he knew the similar works of Michael Haydn. Mozart's first quintet, scored for 2 violins, 2 violas, cello, was written in 1773. He did not use the form again until fourteen years later when his style had reached maturity.

B. K. 174 in B-flat major (1773)

1. The first two movements are written in Italian style; the last two were revised after Mozart became acquainted with the works of Michael Haydn; the work is stylistically uneven.

C. K. 515 in C major; K. 516 in G minor (1787) (*M* 1, p. 135)

1. These two quintets form a pair; strongly contrasted in key (C major and G minor) and mood. The writing is generally for two *concertante* groups. These may be violins and first viola against violas and cello (the first viola belonging to both groups), or violin and cello against the other instruments.

2. The Quintet in C major is light in tone quality. The first movement (Allegro) is in sonata-form with all sections extended and with certain "romantic" tendencies (main theme repeated immediately in the key of the parallel minor, followed by a modulation to A-flat major). The last movement has a development section between the themes in the recapitulation and several instances of enharmonic modulation.

3. The Quintet in G minor is more somber, even though it ends in G major. The theme of the first movement is chromatic, and like the C major quintet has both first and last movements extended.

D. K. 593 in D major (1790); K. 614 in E-flat major (1791) (*M* 1, pp. 162, 174)

1. The last two quintets show a stricter concentration of thematic material and a more contrapuntal texture. Also it is more "romantic" in harmony and modulations.

2. Quintet K. 593 in D major has a slow introduction (Larghetto) before an Allegro; the second subject is a canonic variation of the first. The last movement is full of contrapuntal devices. In the Recapitulation the main subject serves as a counterpoint to the second subject.

3. Quintet K. 614 in E-flat major also has a contrapuntal last movement. Rondo-type with development passages instead of new themes; full of fugatos, inverions, etc.

   a. The first movement is somewhat contrapuntal with busy trills and sixteenth notes. The second theme (meas. 39) is answered by the cello (meas. 46). The Development is relatively short.

   b. The Andante makes use of a combination of *concertante* and chamber music elements. "A combination of brilliance, workmanship, repose and joy in creation."

   c. The Minuet, with a bagpipe Trio, is in the style of Haydn, as is also the Finale.

VII. Trios and Duos

A. K. 266 in B-flat major for 2 violins, cello (1776)

1. A duet for two violins with *continuo*; two movements: Adagio and Minuet.

SALEM COLLEGE SCHOOL OF MUSIC

B. Divertimento K. 563 in E-flat major for violin, viola, cello (1788) (*M* 1, p. 229)
   1. A typical Divertimento, with six movements, two of which are minuets. The writing is mostly in strict three-part style, without double stops.
C. Two Duos K. 423 in G major, K. 424 in B-flat major for violin and viola (1783)
   1. Three movements each; the viola often uses double stops; both instruments share in thematic material. These are said to have been written for Michael Haydn.

VIII. Piano with Other Instruments

A. Trios with Piano
   1. Trios for piano. violin and cello
      a. K. 254 in B-flat major (1776) (*M* 1, p. 278)
         1) Little more than a piano sonata with string accompaniment. The violin rarely has melodic material, usually lies below the right hand of the piano part. The cello generally doubles the piano bass.
      b. K. 442 in D minor (1783)
         1) More advanced in the style of the string parts; finished by Mozart's friend Anton Stadler. Three movements, the last is in the key of the parallel major.
      c. K. 496 in G major, K. 502 in B-flat major (1786) (*M* 1, pp. 271, 245)
         1) Written in the same year as the "Hoffmeister" quartet and in the same period as the three great violin sonatas.
         2) The cello is more important; a tendency toward virtuosity in the piano parts. Both have three movements.
      d. K. 542 in E major, K. 548 in C major, K. 564 in G major (1788)
         1) These usually begin with the piano alone; develop themes of secondary importance; have virtuoso piano parts; consist of three movements. The Trio K. 564 was originally intended as a piano sonata. (*M* 1, pp. 259, 253, 266)
   2. K. 498 in E-flat major (1786) (*M* 1, p. 239)
      a. Trio for piano, clarinet, viola. The work is based on contrast between the viola and clarinet; consists of three movements.
B. Quartets with Piano
   1. K. 478 in G minor (1785), K. 493 in E-flat major (1786) (*M* 1, pp. 93, 102)
      a. The first quartets with piano in real chamber-music style. Both have three movements: Allegro in sonata-form; a slow movement in sonata-form; a typical Mozart Rondo (A - B - A - C - B - A).
C. Quintet for Piano and Winds, K. 452 in E-flat major (1784) (*M* 1, p. 212)
   1. Mozart wrote six piano concertos in 1784, and the quintet reflects the concerto in its virtuoso piano part.
   2. The winds include oboe, clarinet, horn, bassoon. In *concertante* style, with the piano against the wind instruments. The wind group itself is divided into various *concertante* groups.
   3. Three movements: the opening Allegro is preceded by a Largo introduction. The Rondo finale has a concerto-like cadenza played by all instruments. Mozart wrote his father that it was "the best work I have ever composed."

IX. String and Wind Instruments

A. Five Divertimenti
   1. The basic instrumentation is a string quartet and two horns. Two divertimenti add another instrument to this. The Divertimenti are much lighter than other chamber music; often written to celebrate some special occasion. All except one (K. 251) have six movements, including two minuets. The slow movements usually omit the horns. The first violin is definitely a virtuoso instrument. Four of the divertimenti are to be pre-

ceded and followed by a March, which the players performed as they entered and left the room. Divertimento K. 287 was written for a winter performance, so has no March.

   2.   "Vienna" Divertimento, K. 205 in D major (1773)

      a.   A bassoon is added, doubling the cello part. The key of D major is used for all except the slow movement. The March K. 290 precedes and follows the six movements.

   3.   "Salzburg" Divertimenti, K. 247 in F major; K. 287 in B-flat major; K. 334 in D major (1776-1777)

      a.   K. 247 added the March K. 248. K. 334 is also to be played with a March, possibly K. 445. In K. 251, which adds an oboe to the instrumentation, the March is inscribed "*Marcia illa francese.*" K. 287 has for its last movement a Rondo built on the south German popular song "*Die Bauerin hat die Katz verlorn.*" This is preceded and followed by comic recitative, a parody on operatic style.

B.   Four Quartets for Flute, Violin, Viola, Cello: K. 285 in D major; K. 285a in G major; K. 285b in C major (Anhang 171); K. 298 in A major (1777-1778) (*M* 1, pp. 115, 112)

   1.   Mozart was commissioned by a rich amateur flute player to write three quartets with flute. Only the first of the three was complete (K. 285 in D major). The flute part is prominent, but only in the second movement is it a solo instrument. This movement, Adagio, has an accompaniment of pizzicato strings. The unfinished quartets K. 285a and K. 285b (Anhang 171), have only two movements.

   2.   K. 298, in three movements, is a parody on the "foreign" music of his time.

C.   Quartet for Oboe, Violin, Viola, Cello, K. 370 in F major (1781) (*M* 1, p. 119)

   1.   Composed for the oboist Friedrich Ramm of Mannheim in the year of *Idomeneo*. One of Mozart's best works. In three movements; the slow movement has a short cadenza for oboe; in the final Rondo the oboe is sometimes in 4/4 and the other instruments in 6/8 (meas. 95).

D.   Two quintets

   1.   Quintet for Horn, Violin, 2 Violas, Cello, K. 407 in E-flat major (1783) (*M* 1, p. 205)

      a.   In three movements, each in a different style. In the first movement the horn and violin are more in the nature of solo instruments; the other strings act as an accompaniment. The second movement is semi-contrapuntal; short canonic passages throughout. The final Rondo has a virtuoso part for the horn; suggests concerto style, with horn solos and tutti passages.

   2.   Quintet for Clarinet and String Quartet, K. 581 in A major (1789) (*M* 1, p. 194)

      a.   More in chamber style than the horn quintet. Four movements; the Minuet has two Trios, the first Trio omits the clarinet; the last movement is an air and variations instead of a Rondo.

E.   Sonata for Bassoon and Cello, K. 292 in B-flat major (1775)

   1.   Three movements. The instruments are not treated equally; the cello is given a secondary place.

X. Wind Instruments

A.   Twelve Duets for Two Horns, K. 487 (1786)

   1.   Formerly thought to be for two basset horns. Slight, though tuneful, little pieces with the following titles: 1) Allegro, 2) Minuet, 3) Andante, 4) Polonaise, 5) Larghetto, 6) Minuet, 7) Adagio, 8) Allegro, 9) Minuet, 10) Andante, 11) Minuet, 12) Allegro.

B.   Five Divertimenti for Two Clarinets and Bassoon, K. Anhang 229 (1783-1785)

   1.   Slight works; in the key of B-flat major; all have five movements; the first three have the same general form: Allegro - Minuet - Slow movement - Minuet - Rondo. The last two have only one Minuet; No. 4 has two slow movements; No. 5 has a Polonaise and a Romanze for the last two movements. There is little key change between the move-

ments; only one movement in each Divertimento is in a different key; this key is always the key of the dominant or subdominant.

C. Miscellaneous works with Basset Horn
    1. Canonic Adagio for Two Basset Horns and Bassoon, K. 410 in F major (1782)
        a. A very short work. The bassoon is merely an accompanying part; the canon is between the basset horns.
    2. Adagio for Two Clarinets and Three Basset Horns, K. 411 in F major (1782)
        a. Sonata-form. In *concertante* style; the upper four instruments are in various combinations against the third basset horn.

SELECTED BIBLIOGRAPHY

Books

1. Biancolli, Louis P., ed. *The Mozart Handbook; A Guide to the Man and His Music*. Cleveland: World Publishing Co., 1954.
2. Blom, Eric. *Mozart*. New York: E. P. Dutton and Co., 1944.
3. Breakspeare, Eustace John. *Mozart*. New York: E. P. Dutton and Co., 1902; London: J. M. Dent, 1902.
4. Burk, John N. *Mozart and His Music*. New York: Random House, 1959. (Chamber Music: pp. 352-369; 388-403)
5. Deutsch, Otto E. *Mozart, A Documentary Biography*, tr. Eric Blom, Peter Branscombe, Jeremy Noble. Stanford, CA: Stanford University Press, 1966.
6. Dunhill, Thomas F. *Mozart's String Quartets*, Books I and II. New York: Oxford University Press, 1927.
7. Einstein, Alfred. *Mozart: His Character, His Work*, tr. Arthur Mendel and Nathan Broder. New York: Oxford University Press, 1945.
8. Gill, George R. and Murray J. Gould. *A Thematic Locator for Mozart's Works as Listed in Koechel's Chronologisch-Thematisches Verzeichnis*, 6th edition. Hackensack, NJ: Joseph Boonin, 1970.
9. Hutchings, Arthur. *Mozart: The Man, The Musician*. New York: Schirmer Books, 1976.
10. Jahn, Otto. *Wolfgang Amadeus Mozart*, 3 volumes, tr. Pauline D. Townsend. London: Novello and Co., 1891. (reprint: New York: Edwin F. Kalmus)
11. Kenyon, Max. *A Mozart Letter Book*. Westport, CT: Associated Booksellers, 1956.
12. Kerst, Friedrich. *Mozart, the Man and the Artist Revealed in His Own Words*, tr. Henry E. Krehbiel. New York: Dover Publications, 1965.
13. King, A. Hyatt. *Mozart in Retrospect*. London: Oxford University Press, 1955.
14. Köchel, Ludwig Ritter von. *Wolfgang Amade Mozarts Chronologisch-thematisches Verzeichnis sämtlicher Tonwerke*. Wiesbaden: Brietkopf & Härtel, 1964.
15. Landon, H. C. Robbins, and Donald Mitchell. *The Mozart Companion*. London: Oxford University Press, 1956.
16. *The Letters of Mozart and His Family*, 2nd ed., tr. Emily Anderson. New York: St. Martin's Press, 1966.
17. Mersmann, Hans. *Letters of Mozart*, tr. M. M. Bozman. London: J. M. Dent, 1928. (reprint: New York: Dover Publications, 1972)
18. Newman, Ernest W. *A Musical Critic's Holiday*. New York: Alfred A. Knopf, 1925. (pp. 143-150)
19. Niemetschek, Franz. *Life of Mozart* [1798], tr. Helen Mautner. London: Leonard Hyman, 1956.
20. Raynor, Henry B. *Mozart*. London: Macmillan, 1978.
21. Rosen, Charles. *The Classical Style: Haydn, Mozart, Beethoven*. New York: Viking Press,

1971. (Mozart: String Quintets, pp. 264-287)

22. Schenk, Erich. *Mozart and His Times*, tr. Richard and Clara Winston. New York: Alfred A. Knopf, 1959.
23. Talbot, John Edward. *Mozart*. London: Duckworth, 1934; New York: A. A. Wyn, 1949.
24. Tenschert, Roland. *Wolfgang Amadeus Mozart*, tr. Emily Anderson. New York: Macmillan, 1953.
25. Turner, Walter James. *Mozart, the Man and His Work*, 2nd ed., ed. Christopher Raeburn. New York: Barnes and Noble, 1966.
26. Wilder, Victor. *Mozart, the Man and the Artist*, 2 volumes, tr. Louise Liebich. New York: Scribner & Son, 1908.

Articles

1. Beechey, Gwilym E. "Rhythmic Interpretation; Mozart, Beethoven, Schubert, Schumann." *MR* 33 (1972), pp. 233-248.
2. Brown, Maurice. "Mozart's Recapitulations: A Point of Style." *ML* 30 (1949), pp. 109-117.
3. Clapham, John. "Chromaticism in the Music of Mozart." *MR* 17 (1956), pp. 7-18.
4. Cone, Edward T. "Communications [Quartet for piano and strings, K. 478, Mozart]." *PNM* 1, No. 2 (1963), pp. 206-210.
5. Dawson, R. V. "Haydn and Mozart." *MQ* 16 (1930), pp. 498-509.
6. Einstein, Alfred. "Mozart's Choice of Keys," tr. Arthur Mendel. *MQ* 27 (1941), pp. 415-421.
7. ——————"Mozart's Four String Trio Preludes to Fugues of Bach." *MT* 77 (1936), p. 209.
8. ——————"Mozart's Ten Celebrated String Quartets." *MR* 3 (1942), pp. 159-169.
9. ——————"Mozartiana and Köcheliana." *MR* 1 (1940), pp. 313-342; 2 (1941), pp. 68-77; 151-158; 235-242; 324-331.
10. Girdlestone, Cuthbert M. "Mozart's Last Salzburg Compositions." *Chesterian* 16 (1934), p. 29.
11. Grave, Floyd K. "Interpretation through Style Analysis [Mozart, String Quartet in D minor, K. 421]." *College Mus* 18 (1978), pp. 56-71.
12. Hutchings, Arthur. "The Unexpected in Mozart." *ML* 20 (1939), pp. 21-31.
13. Keller, Hans. "Pondering over Mozart's Inconsistencies [String Quartet in B-flat major, K. 589]." *Monthly Musical Record* 89 (May-June 1959), pp. 103-106.
14. ——————"Wordless Functional Analysis No. 1." *Score* 22 (Feb 1958), pp. 56-64.
15. King, A Hyatt. "The Fragmentary Works of Mozart." *MT* 81 (1940), p. 401.
16. ——————"Mozart's Counterpoint: Its Growth and Significance." *ML* 26 (1945), pp. 12-20.
17. ——————"Mozart's Prussian Quartets in Relation to His Later Style." *ML* 21 (1940), pp. 328-246.
18. ——————"A Survey of Recent Mozart Literature." *MR* 3 (1942), pp. 248-258.
19. Lang, Paul Henry. "Mozart after 200 Years." *JAMS* 13 (1960), pp. 197-205.
20. Leavis, Ralph. "Mozart's Flute Quartet in C, K. App. 171." *ML* 43 (1962), pp. 48-52.
21. Leeson, Daniel N., and David Whitwell. "Mozart's 'spurious' Wind Octets." *ML* 53 (1972), pp. 377-399.
22. Lowinsky, Edward E. "On Mozart's Rhythm [Comparison of Haydn's Phrase Structure with Mozart's]." *MQ* 42 (1956), pp. 162-186.
23. McNaught, W. "Mozart's String Quartets. A New Edition." *MT* 86 (1945), p. 235.
24. Mozart, Wolfgang Amadeus. "Mozart's Letters." *British Musician* 5 (1929), p. 10.
25. Newman, Sidney. "Mozart's G minor Quintet (K. 516) and Its Relationship to the G minor Symphony (K. 550)." *MR* 17 (1956), pp. 285-303.
26. Oldman, Cecil Bernard. "Representative Books about Mozart." *ML* 6 (1925), pp. 128-136.

27. Phillips, Harold D. "The Anomalous Place of Mozart in Music." *MQ* 8 (1922), pp. 372-376.
28. Prod'homme, Jacques-Gabriel. "The Wife of Mozart: Constanze Weber," tr. Theodore Baker. *MQ* 13 (1927), pp. 384-409.
29. Schmid, Ernst Fritz. "Mozart and Haydn [Their Influence on Each Other]." *MQ* 42 (1956), pp. 145-161.
30. Tangeman, Robert S. "Mozart's Seventeen Epistle Sonatas." *MQ* 32 (1946), pp. 588-601.
31. Tyson, Alan. "New Light on Mozart's 'Prussian' Quartets." *MT* 116 (1975), pp. 126-130.
32. Vanson, Frederic. "Mozart and the String Quintet––Some Reflections." *Strad* 86 (Mar 1976), p. 815.
33. Vertrees, Julie A. "Mozart's String Quartet K. 465; the History of a Controversy [Clarinet Quintet, K. 581]." *Current Mus* 17 (1974), pp. 96-114.
34. Ward, Martha Kingdon. "Mozart and the Clarinet." *ML* 28 (1947), pp. 126-153.
35. –––––––"Mozart and the Flute." *ML* 35 (1954), pp. 294-308.
36. Watson, J. Arthur. "Mozart and the Viola." *ML* 22 (1941), pp. 41-53.

Music

Study (Miniature) Scores

1. *The Chamber Music of Mozart*, ed. Albert E. Wier. Melville, NY: Belwin-Mills, 1973.
2. String Quartets: *EE* P16, P17; 10 quartets, *Ph* 327-336.
3. String Quartet in D minor, K. 421: *BH* 176.
4. String Quartet in B-flat major, K. 458: *BH* 177.
5. String Quartet in A major, K. 464: *BH* 178.
6. String Quartet in C major, K. 465: *BH* 179.
7. String Quartet in D major, K. 499: *BH* 242.
8. Piano Quartets, K. 478, K. 493: *EE* 159; *Lea* 90.
9. Quartet for oboe, violin, viola, cello, K. 370: *BH* 256; *EE* 194.
10. Quintet for piano, oboe, clarinet, horn, bassoon, K. 452: *EE* 160.
11. Quintet for horn, violin, two violas, cello, K. 407: *EE* 347.
12. Quintet for clarinet and strings, K. 581: *BH* 175.

Playing Parts and Scores

13. String Quartets: *CE*, Series 14; *MNW*, Series 8, *Wg.* 20; *PE* 16, 17 (complete in 2 volumes).
14. *Ten Famous Quartets* for 2 violins, viola and violoncello. Kassel: Bärenreiter, 1964; New York: E. F. Kalmus.
15. String Quintets: *CE*, Series 13; *MNW*, Series 8, *Wg.* 19; *PE* 18, 19 (complete in two volumes).
16. Piano Trios: *CE*, Series 17; *MNW*, Series 2, *Wg.* 22; *PE*, 193 (complete); Munich: G. Henle Verlag, 1972.
17. Piano Quartets K. 478, K. 493: *CE*, Series 17; *MNW*, Series 8, *Wg.* 22; *PE* 272.
18. Three Quartets for flute, violin, viola, cello: *MNW*, Series 8, *Wg.* 20; *PE* 17a.
19. Quintet for horn, violin, two violas, cello, K. 407: *CE*, Series 13; *MNW*, Series 8, *Wg.* 19; New York: International Music Company.
20. Quintet for clarinet and strings, K. 581: *CE*, Series 13; *MNW*, Series 8, *Wg.* 19; New York: International Music Company.

21. *Nineteen Sonatas for Violin & Piano*. New York: International Music Company, 1947.

22. (*CE*) *W. A. Mozart sämtliche Werke*, in 24 Series in 75 volumes. Leipzig: Breitkopf & Härtel, 1877-1905. (reprint: New York: E. F. Kalmus)

23. (*MNW*) *Neue Ausgabe sämtlicher Werke*. Kassel: Bärenreiter, in progress.

24. *Complete String Quartets*. New York: Dover Publications. (reprint: Breitkopf & Härtel)

25. *Complete String Quintets with the Horn and Clarinet Quintets*. New York: Dover Publications. (reprint: Breitkopf & Härtel)

26. *17 Divertimenti for Various Instruments*. New York: Dover Publications, 1979.

27. *10 Divertiment*, ed. G. Nottebohm. New York: Omega Music.

OUTLINE IV

LUDWIG VAN BEETHOVEN (1770 - 1827)

I. **Life**

1770	Born in Bonn, December 16.
1775	Lessons on clavier and violin from his father, a singer in the Electoral choir in Bonn, and local teachers. His father hoped to develop an infant prodigy like Mozart.
1778	Gave first concert in Cologne; advertised as "six years old."
1781	Lessons with Christian Gottlob Neefe; began to compose. Became substitute organist for Neefe at the Electoral Chapel (1782).
1783	Appointed harpsichord and viola player in the court orchestra and accompanist at the theatre (without salary); opportunity to learn new music in various fields.
1784	Appointed assistant court organist (with salary) in addition to other duties. Studied violin with Franz Ries (1785).
1787	Visited Vienna; played for Mozart and received a few lessons. His mother's death left Beethoven to take care of his two brothers and an intemperate father. Met Haydn on his visit to Bonn (1790).
1792	Haydn's second visit to Bonn. Beethoven accepted by Haydn as a pupil; later sent to Vienna by the Elector to study with Haydn. Father died; many personal difficulties arose. Success as a piano virtuoso and teacher.
1794	Began lessons with Johann Georg Albrechtsberger when Haydn went to London. Learned vocal style with Antonio Salieri, an opera composer; quartet writing from Aloys Förster. Soon became his own teacher. Success as a composer.
1798	First signs of deafness appeared. By 1801 he realized that his career as a performer would soon be over.
1803-1815	Composed many of his great works; symphonies (Nos. 3-8), sonatas, chamber music, etc. Many unsuccessful love affairs.
1816-1820	Trouble over his nephew Karl. Few works composed between 1816-1818; after that a new style appeared.
1827	Died March 26; buried in Central Friedhof, Vienna, beside Haydn, Mozart, Gluck, Schubert and Wolf.

II. **Catalogue of Chamber Music (arrangements are not included)**

   A. String Instruments
      1. Quartets
         a. Seventeen for 2 violins, viola, cello (including *Grosse Fuge*)
         b. One string quartet arranged (1802) from the Piano Sonata in E major, Op. 14, No. 1 (1799)
      2. Trios
         a. Five for violin, viola, cello
      3. Quintets
         a. One for 2 violins, 2 violas, cello
         b. One fugue for 2 violins, 2 violas, cello
   B. Piano with other instruments
      1. Sonatas

      a.   Ten for piano, violin
      b.   Five for piano, cello
      c.   One for piano, horn
  2. Trios
      a.   Eight for piano, violin, cello
      b.   One for piano, clarinet, cello
      c.   One for piano, flute, bassoon
  3. Quartets
      a.   Three for piano, violin, viola, cello
  4. Quintet
      a.   One for piano, oboe, clarinet, bassoon, horn (also for piano quartet)
  C. Strings with wind instruments
    1. Trios
      a.   Serenade for flute, violin, viola
    2. Sextet
      a.   One for 2 violins, viola, cello, 2 horns
    3. Septet
      a.   One for violin, viola, clarinet, cello, bassoon, horn, double-bass
  D. Wind Instruments
    1. Duos
      a.   Three for clarinet, bassoon
    2. Trios
      a.   One for 2 oboes, English horn
    3. Quartets
      a.   Three *Equale* for 4 trombones
    4. Sextet
      a.   One for 2 clarinets, 2 horns, 2 bassoons
    5. Octet
      a.   One for 2 oboes, 2 clarinets, 2 horns, 2 bassoons
      b.   *Rondino* for 2 oboes, 2 clarinets, 2 bassoons, 2 horns

III. Chamber Music

  A. Beethoven's compositions are usually divided into three periods:
    1. 1785-1800: influence of the music of Haydn, Mozart and Johann Schobert of the Mannheim School. "Period of imitation."
    2. 1800-1816: the human, mature composer. "Period of externalization."
    3. 1816-1827: development of a new style, high above material considerations. "Period of reflection."
  B. Chamber music was composed throughout his life. Includes about fifty works, not including arrangements. The earliest works were three quartets for piano and strings, composed in Bonn, 1785. His last work was a quartet movement.
    1. Characteristic devices began to appear in compositions of the early Vienna period (1792-1800); themes constructed out of repetitions of a short rhythmic motive; elaborate codas; principle of thematic development; expansion of harmonic scheme; third relationships; sudden modulations.
    2. After 1800 his works generally became more powerful, with greater contrasts in texture and themes, and even more harmonic freedom.
    3. In his last period (1816-1827) his music became sublimated, and new and unusual forms, style and modes of expression appeared.

IV. String Quartets: First Period (1798-1801)

SALEM COLLEGE SCHOOL OF MUSIC

A. Six Quartets, Op. 18: No. 1 in F major, No. 2 in G major, No. 3 in D major, No. 4 in C minor, No. 5 in A major, No. 6 in B-flat major
  1. Dedicated to Prince Joseph Francis von Lobkowitz, one of Beethoven's patrons. Published in sets of three by Tranquillo Mollo in 1801. Chronological order according to composition: No. 3, No. 1, No. 2, No. 5, No. 6, No. 4. First symphony completed in 1799.
  2. The first violin is often given special emphasis; the second violin and viola are subordinated; the cello provides a harmonic bass.
    a. Short, simple, diatonic, rhythmic motives are usually the basis for the first movements.
    b. Slow movements are generally ornate; frequently longer than with Haydn or Mozart; themes in regular phrases.
    c. Third movements are usually very fast.
    d. The texture is generally more harmonic than contrapuntal; all four instruments rarely have separate contrapuntal lines. The Quartets are not related, but all show mastery of form, new techniques and consistent style. There are many sudden contrasts in rhythm and dynamics.
B. Op. 18, No. 1 in F major (*M* 1, p. 8)
  1. Allegro con brio in F major
    a. This shows Beethoven's skill at working out a rhythmic motive, which appears over 100 times in 303 measures. Introduced in unison; treated in imitation, as sequence, as an accompanied melody, and contrapuntally.
    b. Sonata-form. Development (meas. 115-178) uses the theme in imitation and in various keys. Recapitulation (meas. 179-313).
  2. Adagio affettuoso ed appassionato in D minor
    a. Sonata-form: Exposition (meas. 1-45); second theme (meas. 26); Development (meas. 46-62); Recapitulation (meas. 63-95); Coda (meas. 96-110).
  3. Scherzo and Trio: Allegro molto in F major
    a. A fast Minuet in Haydn style. The melody modulates to the dominant; this is repeated and then leads to a contrasting section (meas. 11-36) modulating through A-flat major, F minor, D-flat major, F minor, ending on dominant harmony. It then returns to the principal theme; the second part is much longer than in the usual Scherzo form.
    b. The Trio is built on the contrast of two themes: 1) a leaping octave passage in unison and 2) a running scale passage for the first violin.
  4. Allegro in F major
    a. Sonata-Rondo form. A (meas. 1-42) - B (meas. 43-90) - A (meas. 91-102) - Development (meas. 103-234) - A (meas. 235-278) - B (meas. 279-326) - A and Coda (meas. 327-381).
C. Op. 18, No. 2 in G major (*M* 1, p. 18)
  1. Allegro in G major
    a. Begins immediately with the principal theme, which consists of three short motives. Sectional treatment in conversational style. Exposition (meas. 1-81), second theme (meas. 36); Development (meas. 82-144); Recapitulation (meas. 145-232); Coda (meas. 233-248).
  2. Adagio cantabile in C major
    a. In ternary song form. The cantabile melody of twenty-six measures is followed by an Allegro in F major (meas. 27-58), then a return to the first section with rich ornamentation (meas. 59-86).
  3. Scherzo: Allegro in G major
    a. A lively eight-measure melody built on a rising four-note motive.
  4. Allegro molto quasi Presto in G major
    a. Sonata-form. The first theme is built on a chordal figure D - G - B, announced by

the cello. Development (meas. 82-144); Recapitulation (meas. 145-232); Coda (meas. 233-248).

D. Op. 18, No. 3 in D major. The first quartet of Op. 18 to be written. (*M* 1, p. 26)
   1. Allegro in D major
      a. Shows the influence of Haydn and Mozart. The first theme is a treatment in free imitation of the opening phrases. The second theme (meas. 51) introduces a new rhythm. The Development (meas. 108-158) section is short; begins like the Exposition, but in minor.
   2. Andante con moto in B-flat major
      a. Begins with first and second violins on the fourth string. The slow movement, with its extended Development, is the central point of the whole quartet.
   3. Scherzo and Trio: Allegro in D major
      a. An unusual movement. No literal repetition of the *Maggiore* section after the Trio. The section starts out as usual and is then extended. The two violins are transferred to a higher register and a different key.
   4. Presto in D major
      a. Sonata-form. Vigorous gigue-like rhythm throughout. Second theme (meas. 56); Development (meas. 114-210); Recapitulation (meas. 210).

E. Op. 18, No. 4 in C minor (*M* 1, p. 35)
   1. Allegro ma non tanto in C minor
      a. Begins with a soft, expressive melody. The transition (meas. 13-33) begins with a crash of alternate tonic and dominant chords, leading to a strenuous passage on a dominant pedal. The entrance of the second theme is delayed until measure 34.
   2. Scherzo: Andante scherzoso in C major
      a. Sonata-form with fugal expositions. The second theme is used in canonic imitation. Not a typical scherzo. Principal section (meas. 1-42); subsidiary section (meas. 43-67); closing section (meas. 67-82); Development (meas. 83-145).
   3. Menuetto: Allegretto in C minor
      a. The first theme, a rising melody, makes use of syncopation.
   4. Allegro - Prestissimo in C minor
      a. Rondo form: A - B - A - C - A - B - A. The main theme and both episodes are presented as separate sections, enclosed within double bars. This quartet is more symphonic than any of the others in Op. 18.

F. Op. 18, No. 5 in A major (*M* 1, p. 43)
   1. Allegro in A major
      a. Principal section (meas. 1-24); subsidiary section (meas. 25-55); closing section (meas. 55-79). The first phrase of the theme is the ascending scale of A major. The design and development suggest influences of Mozart.
   2. Menuetto in A major
      a. Begins with a violin melody, taken up later by the viola. The Trio is in binary form.
   3. Andante cantabile in D major
      a. Variation form in the style of Mozart. Five variations, the last one leading to the Coda.
   4. Allegro in A major
      a. Sonata-form. A motive is the basic idea. The second theme is a contrasting slow chordal passage (meas. 36); closing section (meas. 71-94). Recapitulation begins in measure 168; Coda (meas. 264).

G. Op. 18, No. 6 in B-flat major (*M* 1, p. 51)
   1. Allegro con brio in B-flat major
      a. A dialogue between the first violin and cello; the viola and second violin accompany. The second idea enters at measure 44. Development section from measure 92-152. The last chord of the Development is an open fifth (meas. 174).
   2. Adagio ma non troppo in E-flat major

       a.   Extended and elaborated ternary song form with Coda in the tonic.

   3.   Scherzo: Allegro in B-flat major

       a.   Remarkable use of syncopation. One of the most original movements of Op. 18. The Trio is in the style of Haydn; the first violin is prominent.

   4.   *La Malinconia*: Adagio - Allegretto quasi Allegro in B-flat major

       a.   A note at the beginning of this movement indicates that "this piece is to be played with the utmost delicacy."

       b.   Allegretto section in Rondo form: A (meas. 45-76) - B (meas. 77-104) - A^1 (meas. 105-149) - B^1 (meas. 150-181) - A^2 (meas. 182-194) - C (meas. 195-211) - A^3 with a short development and Coda (meas. 212-296).

V.   String Quartets: Second Period (1806-1810)

   A.   Quartets Op. 59: No. 1 in F major, No. 2 in E minor, No. 3 in C major; Op. 74 in E-flat major; Op. 95 in F minor

     1.   The quartets of the second period (1806-1810) are written with complete technical mastery. The style shows frequent expressive contrasts; use of dialogue between instruments; alternation of rhythmic motives; symphonic tendencies in the final movements; emphasis on the main musical idea; diatonic themes; extensive use of thematic development; more use of counterpoint; more virtuoso writing for instruments; higher organization of form; extensive use of sonata-form which is expanded and given freer treatment.

       a.   Op. 59, known as the "Razumovsky Quartets," were commissioned by the Russian Count Andrei Razumovsky. They are related by the use of Russian folk songs (Nos. 1 and 2) and inner content.

   B.   Op. 59, No. 1 in F major (1806) (*M* 1, p. 59)

     1.   Allegro in F major

       a.   Two motives, announced by the cello in the first four measures, build up the first movement. Contrapuntal treatment is used in the Development.

     2.   Allegretto vivace e sempre scherzando in B-flat major

       a.   Sonata-form. Begins with dialogue between the cello and second violin. The first motive is a rhythmic figure on one note, which recurs throughout. Dynamics range from *p* to sudden *ff*; melodic sections break off into others with great leaps; unexpected modulations; sudden contrasts.

     3.   Adagio molto e mesto in F minor

       a.   Sonata-form, but second theme (meas. 24) is modified and elaborated on its return.

     4.   Thème Russe: Allegro in F major

       a.   Sonata-form with Rondo characteristics. No break between the third and fourth movements. Begins in F major, modulates to D minor, then to C major, introducing the second theme (meas. 45). The Russian melody enters in C minor. The Development section uses thematic development (meas. 100-178).

   C.   Op. 59, No. 2 in E minor (*M* 1, p. 74)

     1.   Allegro in E minor

       a.   Begins with a tonic and a dominant chord, followed by a measure rest; a short principal theme of Op. 18 type then enters. The Development section uses opening chords as an underlying motive. Modulations in the Development are from E-flat major to B minor, G major, A-flat major, resolving in C major.

     2.   Molto Adagio in E major

       a.   A note in Italian at the beginning of this movement suggests that "This piece must be played with great sentiment."

       b.   Sonata-form (second theme, meas. 27). This begins with a chorale-like section based on two phrases; after repetition in the lower register, a triplet figure appears which continues throughout the movement. The Chorale then progresses from B major to D major, then changes quickly to minor and a modulation is made to B-flat major. The agitated triplet figure continues as before.

    c.   The Chorale passage comes back and begins the Development section; modulates by means of the dominant of A major, goes from major to minor, then to E major. The Chorale theme again enters in all four instruments. The dynamics and register are gradually lowered and the movement ends softly in E major.

3.   Allegretto in E minor (Scherzo)

    a.   Form: A - A^1 - B - B^1 - C - A - B. Unusual rhythmic pattern in the first section; in triple meter with the accent on the second beat, a dotted quarter note.

    b.   The second section is in a quieter mood in G major; modulates to A minor, then F major (using the accented second-beat rhythmic pattern), and E minor. The *Maggiore* section is based on a Russian folk tune. The fugato section uses the melody canonically and sometimes as an accompanied melody.

4.   Finale: Presto in E minor

    a.   Rondo form: A (meas. 1-69) - B (meas. 70-106) - A^1 (meas. 107-145) - Development (meas. 146-215) - B^1 (meas. 216-274) - A^2 and Coda (meas. 275-409). Begins in the key of C major. The first violin carries the melody, with the lower strings playing a rhythmical chordal accompaniment. Modulation to E minor after seven measures with a quick return to C major. The closing "Più presto" section begins in E minor and establishes the fundamental tonality. Much rhythmic movement and massive chordal writing concludes the quartet.

D.   Op. 59, No. 3 in C major   (*M* 1, p. 85)

1.   Andante con moto - Allegro vivace in C minor

    a.   This is the first use of a slow opening section in Beethoven's quartets. The introduction is in triple meter with shifting harmonies, which finally establish the key of the Allegro (C major).

    b.   The first violin opens the Allegro and introduces the principal theme in a typical rhythmic pattern. This is repeated in D minor and ends on the dominant of F major, modulating back to C major. The second theme is also introduced by the first violin (meas. 77). Imitation is freely used in passages which follow. The Development leads to E-flat major and the first theme reappears. The keys passed through are F major, C minor, F major and finally C major. The principal theme then begins the third section of the movement.

2.   Andante con moto quasi Allegretto in A minor

    a.   Sonata-form (second theme, meas. 42). The long melodic line is introduced by the first violin, accompanied by pizzicato cello, which continues without accent or break. Contrary motion between the strings is prominent in the following passage. After the second repeated section, louder dynamics and a higher register are used for contrast. The keys used in the Development are A major, D minor, E-flat major. After the Development the first theme, now modified, enters in E major.

3.   Menuetto: Grazioso in C major

    a.   Some elements of sonata-form. Divided into two sections, the first is not repeated. The first section is chordal and rhythmic; the upper three instruments play in the same note values. The second section is entirely different; the first violin plays a phrase based on the principal motive, accompanied by other instruments. The phrase introduced by the first violin is treated in imitation.

    b.   The Trio begins with an arpeggiated figure based on the F major triad. Divided into two sections: the first ends in C major; the second begins in A major without preparation and then becomes the dominant of D minor. It continues to F major.

4.   Allegro molto in C major

    a.   Sonata-form with fugal principal section. The high point of Op. 59 and an unusually outstanding movement. Fugal style; the subject, which is ten measures long, is introduced by the viola, followed by the second violin, cello and first violin. The subject is used in imitation between the instruments, leading to an episode in E-flat major.

The keys which follow are F minor, D-flat major, C-sharp minor; throughout this section the principal subject is introduced in many modified versions.
  b. Modulations from C-sharp minor to D minor; the section which follows is one of great tension and dramatic power. The first violin then takes a fragment of the opening subject and, with the sforzando chordal accompaniment, builds a powerful climax.
  c. A delay follows on the dominant of C major, then the fugal treatment of the subject begins again. Instruments enter as in the Exposition, but this time a new counter-subject in half notes is used. Material is used with some modification leading to the Coda. The subject is now heard in contrary motion, in short statements.
E. Op. 74 in E-flat major ("The Harp") (1810) (*M* 1, p. 98)
  1. Poco adagio - Allegro in E-flat major
    a. Introduction of twenty-four measures. Downward leap of a prominent figure, occurring nine times. Effective modulatory passages.
    b. The Allegro is linked to the Introduction by a series of energetic chords. The principal theme enters (meas. 27). Pizzicato harp-like accompaniment used in measures 35, 125, 153, 221, 251. The Development is in three sections, built on the principal theme and a thematic figure.
  2. Adagio ma non troppo in A-flat major
    a. Rondo form: A - B - A - C - A - Coda. A long, unbroken melody, introduced by the first violin; less ornamental than Op. 18. The B section comes in (meas. 25) without any transition, leading to the tonic minor; about thirty-six measures of modulatory writing follow.
    b. The A section returns (meas. 64) with a new accompaniment in the inner parts, ending in A-flat major. The C section begins in measure 87. The first violin states the principal theme for the third time (meas. 115), modified in its further restatement. Coda (meas. 139-169); A and B themes appear.
  3. Presto in C minor
    a. Scherzo form with repeated Trio. This is comparable to the Allegro of the Fifth Symphony; uses the same rhythmic figure. A fast scherzo-like movement in A - B - A form with repeated Trio. After opening in C minor, the music goes through several modulations leading into a new section in G minor. Modulations to the dominant of F major, then to F minor, C minor, ending abruptly in C major.
  4. Allegretto con Variazioni in E-flat major
    a. Variation form with six variations, some divided into two sections. Other "partial" variations enter in the Coda.
F. Op. 95 in F minor (1810) "Quartet Serioso" (*M* 1, p. 109)
  1. Op. 95, as well as Op. 74, is transitional in style.
  2. Allegro con brio in F minor
    a. Begins with a strong unison passage announcing the first half of the principal theme. Second half of the first theme is strongly rhythmical. The second theme (meas. 24) is in D-flat major; suggests figures and rhythms of the first theme. Many unprepared modulations and chromatic transitions: G-flat major, F major, D-flat major, A-flat major, A major, D-flat major, D major, D-flat major, A-flat major, F major. The Development treats the principal theme in imitation, then exploits the second half of the theme. The Recapitulation (meas. 83) discards the second half of the theme. The second theme reappears in D-flat major and moves to F major. The rhythmic motive is persistently used in the Coda (meas. 129).
  3. Allegretto ma non troppo in D major
    a. Ternary song form, or Aria form in five sections. Opens with a slow downward scale passage of four measures in length in the cello. The first violin enters at the fifth measure with a long melody made up of several phrases. Harmonic feeling shifts between D major and G minor. The viola announces a theme (meas. 34) which is de-

veloped fugally. Single notes of the cello recur and the section ends on the dominant of D major (meas. 76). The fugato section is repeated. The Recapitulation of Section I begins in measure 112. The fugato theme enters abruptly in the viola (meas. 144). The second phrase of the first melody (meas. 153) enters in the cello. The work ends on a diminished seventh with the introductory idea.

4. Allegro assai vivace ma serioso in F minor
    a. Fast, highly rhythmical Scherzo movement in A - B - A - B - A form; uses contrapuntal devices.
    b. The Trio in G-flat major begins (meas. 40) after the first section (meas. 1-39) has been repeated. A chordal, chorale-like melody in the three lower strings is accompanied by the first violin in a harp-like figure. The cello takes the melody and modulations go through D major and then to B minor.
    c. The first Recapitulation of the Scherzo (meas. 103). The Trio (meas. 145) is in D major instead of G-flat major. Modulations through G major, C minor, F minor. The Scherzo returns in F minor (meas. 183).

5. Larghetto espressivo - Allegretto agitato in F minor and F major
    a. A short, expressive, romantic introduction moves quickly to the agitated Allegretto in Rondo-Sonata form. The first theme is composed of two motives and a concluding phrase. The second theme (intermediate section) enters in the second violin (meas. 44). There is imitation between the viola and cello.
    b. The first section returns, followed by a short Development; the second motive of the first theme is used in close imitation. The second theme (intermediate section) enters in F minor (meas. 94). The first section returns (meas. 95); the first theme is taken by the first violin, accompanied by the lower strings. The Coda (meas. 133) in F major introduces a new theme in the first violin.

VI. String Quartets: Third Period (1824-1826)

A. Quartets Op. 127 in E-flat major; Op. 132 in A minor; Op. 130 in B-flat major; Op. 133 (*Grosse Fuge*); Op. 131 in C-sharp minor, Op. 135 in F major. The Quartets (Op. 127, 132,130) were commissioned by Prince Nicholas von Galitzin, a wealthy Russian amateur cellist. The Third period quartets were composed in the order given above.

B. The style shows continuous organic development; extended melodic lines; use of tones foreign to the key; equal interest among instruments; increased polyphonic complexity; all parts independent; complex part-writing; powerful syncopation; a tendency to use extremely unrelated keys; adaptation of material; use of more than four parts; changing tempos and slow opening sections (except Op. 135).

C. Op. 127 in E-flat major (1824) (*M* 1, p. 118)
    1. Maestoso - Allegro in E-flat major
        a. The movement is mostly contrapuntal; the only homophonic passages are in the Maestoso sections, the two bridge cadences and the two appearances of the second theme. The movement opens with a four-measure melody reminiscent of a Bach subject. The Development begins with the second Allegro (meas. 81-166); includes two statements of the Maestoso section. The Coda is from measure 241 to the end.
    2. Adagio, ma non troppo e molto cantabile in A-flat major
        a. A simple harmonization of a diatonic scale-wise melody followed by five variations. One of Beethoven's finest movements.
    3. Scherzando vivace in E-flat major
        a. The theme is a four-note staccato group; used in all possible ways. Many sudden changes of dynamics and tempo.
    4. Finale in E-flat major
        a. Opens with a four-measure Introduction; a folk-like theme is then announced. An arpeggio motive is introduced and appears in all instruments at different times.
        b. The Development is introduced after a recurrence of the four-measure Introduction.

The second theme enters in C major, then in C minor; then it is used in canon. At the Allegro commodo (6/8), Beethoven subtly and slowly moves to E-flat major; harmonies then change oftener, and finally reach the tonic.

D.   Op. 130 in B-flat major (1825-1826)   (*M* 1, p. 131)

1.   Adagio, ma non troppo - Allegro in B-flat major

    a.   The Adagio is an introduction of fourteen measures. The Development section uses some of this material. At the Allegro, two figures appear, one in sixteenth notes introduced by the first violin, the other in quarter notes introduced by the second violin. These appear frequently in the following measures.

    b.   The Development begins at measure 94 in the key of G-flat major. The key of D major is reached by an enharmonic change of G-flat to F-sharp. There is one measure of Allegro, three measures of Adagio, again one measure of Allegro, three measures of Adagio, and finally Allegro, this time continuing with the quarter-note figure in the first violin and cello. Recapitulation (meas. 132-213). Short Adagios and Allegros reappear in the Coda (meas. 214).

2.   Presto: Scherzo in B-flat minor

    a.   The first section is divided into two parts; each is repeated, ending in B-flat major. The Trio (meas. 17-63) is in two parts, each repeated, followed by a transitory passage leading to a Recapitulation of the Scherzo. The first violin uses a modified principal theme in a sequential manner, accompanied by the lower instruments. This theme appears continuously until the scale passages leading to the ritardando section; all instruments are in dotted half-note rhythm.

    b.   A short solo passage for the first violin appears at the return of the *L'istesso tempo*, followed by a forte unison of all instruments on a three-note staccato figure. This passage is used twice again, differently each time. The first section returns with the melody modified and the use of imitation. The Coda (meas. 96) introduces the principal theme in mirror, with the viola reiterating it in normal position.

3.   Andante con moto, ma non troppo in D-flat major

    a.   Sonata-form: Exposition (meas. 1-25), Development (meas. 29-37), Recapitulation (meas. 38-65). The movement begins in the key of B-flat major. The first theme is introduced by the viola in measure 3 and taken by the first violin an octave higher in measure 5. Interchange of melodic material is followed by free imitation (meas. 20).

    b.   The Cantabile section, with the melody in the first violin (meas. 26) is repeated in simplified form. The Coda begins at measure 66 with the appearance of a pizzicato accompaniment in the lower strings; modulatory passages and unprepared chords lead to a novel conclusion in D-flat major.

4.   Alla danza tedesca: Allegro assai in G major

    a.   Ternary song form in the style of a German dance; originally written for Op. 132. The main section (meas. 1-24) and Trio (meas. 25-80), with customary repetitions, recall an early type of Scherzo. The Recapitulation (meas. 81-128) is followed by the Coda (meas. 129). The germ of the movement is found in the first four measures.

5.   Cavatina: Adagio molto espressivo in E-flat major

    a.   Long, expressive melodic phrase. The first period is nine measures long, repeated but slightly modified and shortened. The second theme enters at measure 23 in the second violin; freely imitated by the first violin. Middle section (meas. 40-49); Recapitulation (meas. 50-66).

6.   Finale: Allegro in B-flat major

    a.   Sonata-Rondo form: A - B - C - Development - Recapitulation - D - A - Coda. In its original form this work concluded with the *Grosse Fuge*, but owing to its extreme length it was replaced in 1825 by this movement and the fugue was published separately as Op. 133.

    b.   This Finale was Beethoven's last work. It opens with the solo viola playing an octave accompaniment figure; the main theme is in the first violin. The entire movement is devoted to the working out of this material; mirroring, imitation and "passing around" of themes. The B section (meas. 67-108) followed by the C section (meas. 109-161).

c. The Development begins at measure 162, the Recapitulation at measure 223, the D section at measure 253 and the final A section at measure 430.

E. Op. 131 in C-sharp minor (1826) (Seven movements played without interruption)
1. Adagio, ma non troppo e molto espressivo in C-sharp minor (*M* 1, p. 144)
   a. The principal theme, introduced by the first violin, is four measures long. It is treated in fugal style with entrances by other instruments every four measures. After the final entrance of the Exposition in the cello, the contrapuntal writing becomes free. There is imitation between the first violin and cello, and the second violin and viola (meas. 21). Much contrapuntal writing follows, with new imitations. Suggestions of *Parsifal* in measures 63-66. The first violin takes the subject from the viola (meas. 99); this is followed by the augmentation of the subject by the cello (meas. 100). Modulation to the tonic, C-sharp minor.
2. Allegro molto vivace in D major
   a. A bright homophonic movement contrasted with a somber first movement. The first violin has the theme, accompanied by sustained passages in the other instruments. The viola takes the theme (meas. 9), then the first violin. The second theme is in measure 24. The music becomes more polyphonic with the "working out" of the rhythmic figuration; an unusual harmonic progression (meas. 66-67). Return of the principal themes, leading without stop to the next section.
3. Allegro moderato - Adagio in B minor
   a. A short recitative-like introduction of eleven measures leads to a theme and variations.
4. Andante, ma non troppo e molto cantabile in A major (Coda in C major)
   a. A theme and seven variations with an extended Coda. The theme is thirty-two measures long, divided between the two violins. It consists of two eight-measure sections, each repeated.
   b. Variation I
      1) The second violin approximates the theme in a different rhythm; the first violin has falling phrases in sixteenth notes. At the repetition, the cello has the falling phrases.
   c. Variation II (Più mosso)
      1) The first half of the theme is used in a duet between the violin and cello. The second half of the theme is used in a modified version. The cello takes the second half at the repetition.
   d. Variation III (Andante moderato e lusinghiero)
      1) This variation begins with a canon at the second between the viola and cello, which is repeated by the violins. The second section (meas. 113) starts with another canon, again between viola and cello. It is later joined by the violins at the repeat.
   e. Variation IV (Adagio)
      1) There is little similarity between this variation and the theme. The motive in measure 3 is used. Passages are accentuated by pizzicato notes; the violins have a duet in thirds, sixths and octaves.
   f. Variation V (Allegretto)
      1) All the instruments begin with double stops. The music is very restrained, based on the harmony of the theme.
   g. Variation VI (Adagio, ma non troppo e semplice)
      1) This begins with a chordal pattern, which is later used an octave higher (meas. 195). The solo ascending scale passage in the first violin (meas. 220) is later given

to the viola, cello and second violin. The first violin takes the scale passage in a descending pattern, leading eventually to Variation VII.

   h.   Variation VII
      1)   Incomplete and in recitative style.
   i.   Coda - Allegretto in C major
      1)   The beginning of the principal theme is stated in country-dance style. Trills are used throughout. There is a display of virtuosity before the sudden close of the movement.

5.   Presto: Scherzo in E major
   a.   The first entrance by the cello is only one measure long, followed by a full measure rest. A short development of the first two measures of the theme. The theme is in G-sharp minor, returning quickly to the original key. This is repeated, and the B theme is introduced (meas. 69); the key changes to A major. The Trio begins (meas. 110) with the rhythm in four-measure phrases. A new theme begins at measure 141. Return to A then B themes; reference to the C theme. The first use of ponticello bowing (close to the bridge) in a quartet (meas. 470).

6.   Adagio quasi un poco andante in G-sharp minor
   a.   The viola introduces the first theme, which is then taken over by the first violin. The theme is heard throughout this short movement, which leads directly to the Finale.

7.   Allegro in C-sharp minor
   a.   Sonata-form. The theme is a group made up of three themes, all of which are developed. Theme A^1 appears in measure 2, A^2 in measures 5-8, A^3 in measure 21 (first violin). The themes are treated contrapuntally in the sections which follow. Part of the fugue theme of the first movement appears in measures 30-31. The Coda uses a melody made up of the three themes, treated in a new way.

F.   Op. 132 in A minor (1824-1825)   (*M* 1, p. 157)
   1.   Assai sostenuto - Allegro in A minor
      a.   The cello introduces the A theme in the first and second measures, mirrored by the viola in measures 3 and 4. This theme appears in various forms in Quartets Op. 132 in A minor, Op. 133 (*Grosse Fuge*), Op. 131 in C-sharp minor. The first theme is suggested by the cello (meas. 11) and played completely by the first violin (meas. 13), then repeated by the cello and continued by the viola. The second theme enters in measure 48.
      b.   The Development begins at measure 75 with the entrance of the cello stating the A theme. The Recapitulation (meas. 119) begins in the key of E minor and follows the Exposition fairly closely. The Coda (meas. 189) follows, passing through the keys of A minor, A major, and ending with a crescendo in A minor.

   2.   Allegro ma non tanto in A major
      a.   A Scherzo and Trio with a *da capo* at the end of the middle section. Restrained in mood. The thematic material is found in measures 5 and 6. The main theme is in the first violin, the B theme in the second violin. The movement opens with the B theme in octaves in all four instruments. The two themes are found in all but five measures of the main section. The Trio begins at measure 120, followed by the da capo.

   3.   Molto adagio - Andante
      a.   "Holy Song of Thanksgiving to the Divinity by a Convalescent, in the Lydian Mode." Form: A - B - A varied - B - A varied - Coda. The adagio section uses a chorale-like tune of five phrases in the Lydian mode. A fragment found in the opening three measures is used in later sections. The andante section ("the invalid feels new strength") (meas. 31) in D major moves vigorously and in contrast to the first section. The theme of this section is in the second violin; repeated in measure 39; the rest of the section is less vigorous and it ends pianissimo. The adagio returns

(meas. 84), and the first violin has the chorale tune an octave higher; less imitation, but more syncopation, especially in the second violin and cello. The Andante reappears (meas. 115) almost as before, except that the violin has the theme, followed later by the second violin. In the third appearance of the Adagio (meas. 168), the first phrase of the chorale tune is used; imitation at different intervals, and at different parts of the measure.

4. Alla marcia, assai vivace in A minor
   a. The first section consists of eight measures repeated. A second section (meas. 9-14) and recapitulation of the first section follows, also repeated. A Recitative, Più Allegro, enters (meas. 25); the first violin has a recitative passage, accompanied by tremolo strings; followed by a solo for first violin (Presto), leading directly to the Finale.
5. Allegro appassionato in A minor
   a. Rondo form: A - B - A - C - A - B - A. The main theme is introduced by the first violin; repeated an octave higher soon after. The B section (meas. 52-59). After the fourth appearance of the main melody, a Coda section in A major introduces two new themes. The first is stated by the cello in high register and repeated by the violins in octaves.

G. Op. 133, *Grosse Fuge* in B-flat major (1825) (*M* 1, p. 169)
   1. Originally written as the last movement of Quartet Op. 130. It begins in G minor; the main theme is asserted by the four instruments (meas. 2-10). The main theme A, which is the basic motive used in Op. 132, appears in various ways in measures 1-10 in G minor, 11-16 modulating to F major, 17-25 in F major, 26-30 in B-flat major. This is called "*Overtura*" in the original manuscript.
   2. Section I (meas. 30-158, B-flat major to G-flat major) uses a new theme B with the main theme A as a countersubject.
   3. Section II, Meno mosso e moderato 2/4 (meas. 159-232, G-flat major to B-flat major), uses the B theme altered.
   4. Section III, Allegro molto e con brio 6/8 (meas. 233-272, B-flat major), uses theme A in Scherzo style.
   5. Section IV (meas. 273-413, A-flat major) expands theme A, which appears in diminution at measure 350.
   6. Section V (meas. 414-662, E-flat major) uses themes A and B, and Sections II (meno mosso, 2/4) and III (Allegro molto, 6/8) return.
   7. Section VI (meas. 663-741, B-flat major), the final section, presents theme A in the tonic with theme B as a countermelody.

H. Op. 135 in F major (1826) (*M* 1, p. 177)
   1. Allegretto
      a. Built on many themes and fragmentary statements. The main theme appears in the first measure, stated by the viola, and is repeated. A new idea appears, played in octaves by the violin and viola (meas. 10). The first violin introduces another theme (meas. 24). A new theme appears in a three-octave unison passage (meas. 46). The closing theme enters at measure 54.
      b. The Development begins with a cello solo (meas. 62); use of triple invertible counterpoint.
      c. There is an unusual use of themes in the Recapitulation (meas. 101-163). Material which follows is a modified version of the main fragments. The Coda (meas. 163) is treated similarly to the Development.
   2. Vivace: Scherzo in F major
      a. Begins with syncopation. The main theme is in the first violin; repeated, after the opening eight measures an octave higher by the second violin. Syncopation follows and the theme returns over a pedal C in the cello (meas. 25). The violin and cello exchange parts which opened the movement (meas. 33).

    b.   The second section is repeated; it leads into the Trio (meas. 67) which uses an ascending scale passage in F major. This returns in G major, then in A major. Three lower instruments have an ostinato of fifty-one measures based on the cello and viola figure (meas. 142) found in the first measure of the Trio.

    c.   The first section returns and repeats; ends with a short Coda.

3.   Lento assai, cantante e tranquillo in D-flat major

    a.   Theme with variations. Opens with a two-measure introduction, followed by an eight-measure melody in the first violin, with sustained accompaniment in the lower strings. Last measure of this phrase repeated by the cello and then by the first violin. First eight measures are varied (meas. 13-20).

    b.   The middle section begins at the Più Lento in C-sharp minor (meas. 23). Returns to the first section at Tempo I (meas. 33). The cello has the main theme, the violin the same theme slightly modified; these two instruments are in canon, the cello following the violin. The Coda (meas. 43) is made up of fragments.

4.   Grave, ma non troppo tratto - Allegro in F major, "Resolution reached with difficulty."

    a.   Sonata-form. The two short themes stated at the beginning, *"Muss es sein?"* and *"Es muss sein!"* are the motivating forces of the whole movement. The viola and cello state the first of the two themes in five of the twelve measures of the Grave. In the first four measures, there is close imitation, of a descending and then ascending figure by the first violin, viola, and second violin. The Allegro begins with the "It must be!" theme, then introduces a new theme in the first violin (meas. 17). This theme is used in close imitation, first in the tonic, then in A major. The second theme begins in measure 53.

    b.   The Development (meas. 81-173) uses the "It must be!" theme modified. A new theme, first used in the Allegro section, is again used in canon (meas. 88), with the addition of the "It must be!" theme appearing in each instrument. The music returns to the Grave section (meas. 161-173); "Must it be?" and "It must be!" themes appear several times.

    c.   The Recapitulation (meas. 174-243) begins with a variation of the "It must be!" theme. The Coda begins at measure 244 with a slow statement of the "It must be!" theme, which is followed by a pizzicato section leading to the close of the movement.

SELECTED BIBLIOGRAPHY

Books

1.   Abraham, Gerald. *Beethoven's Second-Period Quartets*, 2nd ed. London: Oxford University Press, 1943.

2.   Arnold, Denis, and Nigel Fortune. *The Beethoven Reader*. New York: W. W. Norton, 1971. (Chamber Music: pp. 197-278)

3.   Burk, John N. *The Life and Works of Beethoven*. New York: Random House, 1943. (Chamber Music: pp. 345-411)

4.   Fiske, Roger. *Beethoven's Last Quartets*, 3rd ed. London: Oxford University Press, 1948.

5.   Hadow, William Henry. *Beethoven's Op. 18 Quartets*. London: Oxford University Press, 1926.

6.   Kerman, Joseph. *The Beethoven Quartets*. New York: Alfred A. Knopf, 1967. (paperback: New York: W. W. Norton, 1966)

7.   Kerst, Friedrich, and Henry E. Krehbiel, eds. *Beethoven, the Man and the Artist as Revealed in His Own Words*. New York: Dover Publications, 1964. (reprint of 1905 edition)

8. Kinsky, George. *Das Werke Beethovens Thematisch-Bibliographisches Verzeichnis seiner sämtlichen Vollendeten Kompositionen*. Munich: G. Henle Verlag, 1955.
9. Kolodin, Irving. *The Interior Beethoven; a Biography of the Music*. New York: Alfred A. Knopf, 1975.
10. *The Letters of Beethoven*, 3 volumes; tr. Emily Anderson. New York: St. Martin's Press, 1961.
11. Marliave, Joseph de. *Beethoven's Quartets*, tr. Hilda Andrews. New York: Dover Publications, 1961.
12. Mason, Daniel Gregory. *The Quartets of Beethoven*. New York: Oxford University Press, 1947.
13. Nottebohm, Gustav. *Ludwig van Beethoven Thematisches Verzeichnis*. Wiesbaden: Dr. Martin Sändig oHG, 1969.
14. Radcliffe, Philip. *Beethoven's String Quartets*. London: Cambridge University Press, 1978.
15. Rosen, Charles. *The Classical Style: Haydn, Mozart, Beethoven*. New York: Viking Press, 1971.
16. Sadie, Stanley. *Beethoven*. London: Faber & Faber, 1967.
17. Schmidt-Görg, Joseph, and Hans C. Schmidt. *Ludwig van Beethoven*. London: Pall Mall Press, 1970; New York: Praeger Press, 1970.
18. Scott, Marion M. *Beethoven*. London: J. M. Dent, 1960; New York: Farrar, Straus and Cudahy, 1960. (Chamber Music: pp. 230-277)
19. Shepherd, Arthur. *The String Quartets of Ludwig van Beethoven*. Cleveland: Horace Carr, The Printing Press, 1935.
20. Thayer, Alexander Wheelock. *The Life of Ludwig van Beethoven*, ed. Elliot Forbes. Princeton: Princeton University Press, 1967.
21. Tovey, Donald F. *Beethoven*. London: Oxford University Press, 1965.
22. Truscott, Harold. *Beethoven's Late String Quartets*. London: Dennis Dobson, 1968.

Articles

1. d'Aranyi, Jelly. "The Violin Sonatas." *ML* 8 (1927), pp. 191-197.
2. Beechey, Gwilym E. "Rhythmic Interpretation; Mozart, Beethoven, Schubert and Schumann." *MR* 33 (1972), pp. 233-248.
3. Brandenberg, Sieghard. "The First Version of Beethoven's C major String Quartet, Op. 18, No. 2." *ML* 58 (1977), pp. 127-152.
4. Capell, Richard. "Beethoven and His Time." *ML* 8 (1927), pp. 262-267.
5. Clarke, Rebecca. "The Beethoven Quartets as a Player Sees Them." *ML* 8 (1927), pp. 178-190.
6. Colles, Henry C. "Beethoven (1770-1827)." *Music Bulletin* 9 (1927, p. 77.
7. Dunhill, Thomas F. "The Music of Friends: Some Thoughts on the String Quartets of Beethoven." *MT* 68 (1927), p. 113.
8. Cooke, Deryck. "The Unity of Beethoven's Late Quartets." *MR* 24 (1963), pp. 30-49.
9. Dickinson, Alan E. "The Beethoven Quartets." *Mus Opinion* 93 (Apr 1970), p. 357.
10. Dullo, W. A. "The Mysterious Four-Note Motive in Beethoven's Late String Quartets." *Canon* 17, No. 3 (1964), pp. 10-15.
11. Engel, Carl. "Review of Ernest Newman's 'The Unconscious Beethoven'." *MQ* 13 (1927), pp. 646-662.
12. Grew, Sidney. "Beethoven's 'Grosse Fuge'." *MQ* 17 (1931), pp. 497-508.
13. ————"Beethoven's 'Grosse Fuge,' an Analysis." *ML* 12 (1931), pp. 253-261.
14. Hadow, William Henry. "Variation-Form." *ML* 8 (1927), pp. 127-130.
15. Johnson, Douglas. "Beethoven's Sketches for the Scherzo of the Quartet, Op. 18, No. 6." *JAMS* 23 (1970), pp. 385-404.
16. Kerman, Joseph. "Beethoven: the Single Journey [Quartet in A minor, Op. 132]." *Hudson Rev* 5 (1952-1953), pp. 32-55.

17. Kirkendale, Warren. "The 'Great Fugue' Opus 133: Beethoven's 'Art of Fugue'." *Acta Mus* 35 (1963), pp. 14-24.
18. Kolisch, Rudolph. "Tempo and Character in Beethoven's Music," tr. Arthur Mendel. *MQ* 29 (1943), pp. 169-187; 291-312.
19. Kramer, Jonathan D. "Multiple and Non-Linear Time in Beethoven's Opus 135." *PNM* 11, No. 2 (1973), pp. 122-145.
20. Livingstone, Ernest F. "A Structural Analysis of Beethoven's String Quartet in F minor, Op. 95." *JAMS* 8 (1955), p. 226.
21. Lumoa, Robert G. "Variant Dynamic Marking in Music: Some Examples from Mozart and Beethoven [String Quartet, No. 3 in D]." *MR* 34 (1973), pp. 194-197.
22. MacArdle, Donald W. "The Artaria Editions of Beethoven's C major Quintet." *JAMS* 16 (1963), pp. 254-257.
23. ――――"Beethoven, Artaria, and the C Major Quintet." *MQ* 34 (1948), pp. 567-574.
24. ――――"Beethoven's Autographs [Quintet in C, Op. 29]." *MT* 97 (1956), p. 428.
25. McEwen, John B. "Beethoven's Third Period." *ML* 8 (1927), pp. 156-162.
26. Oldman, Cecil Bernard. "A Beethoven Bibliography." *ML* 8 (1927), pp. 276-288.
27. Riseling, Robert A. "Motivic Structures in Beethoven's Late Quartets," in *Paul A. Pisk. Essays in His Honor*, ed. Johan Glowacki. Austin: University of Texas Press, 1966, pp. 141-162.
28. Tovey, Donald F. "Some Aspects of Beethoven's Art Forms." *ML* 8 (1927), pp. 131-155.
29. ――――"The Music Antecedents of Beethoven's Style." *ML* 25 (1944), p. 63.
30. Unger, Max. "From Beethoven's Workshop," tr. Willis Wager. *MQ* 24 (1938), pp. 323-340.
31. Walthew, Richard. "Chamber Music." *ML* 8 (1927), pp. 317-321.
32. Watson, J. Arthur. "Beethoven's Debt to Mozart." *ML* 18 (1937), pp. 248-258.
33. White, F. "Some Notes (and a New Book) on Beethoven's String Quartets." *Chesterian* 8 (Jan-Feb 1927), p. 122.

Music

Study (Miniature) Scores

1. *The Chamber Music of Beethoven*, ed. Albert E. Wier. Melville, NY: Belwin-Mills, 1973.
2. String Trios, Op. 3, 8, 9, Nos. 1-3: *EE*; *KSS* 1006; *Lea* 99.
3. String Quartets, Op. 18, Nos. 1-6: *KSS* 759; *Lea* 61; *Ph* 310-315.
   Op. 59, No. 1-3: *KSS* 760; *Lea* 62; *Ph* 316-318.
   Op. 74, 95, 127, 130: *KSS* 761; *Lea* 63; *Ph* 319-322.
   Op. 131, 132, 133, 135: *KSS* 762; *Lea* 64; *Ph* 323-326.
4. String Quartet, Op. 18, Nos. 2, 3, 4: *BH* 124, 125, 126.
5. String Quartet, Op. 59, No. 3: *BH* 131.
6. String Quartet, Op. 132: *BH* 137.
7. String Quintets, Op. 4, 29, 104, 137: *EE*; *KSS* 1005.
8. Piano Trios: *EE* 79, 82, 83, 122, 123, 124, 223, 278; *KSS* 1013, 1014, 1015, 1016; *Lea* 151, 152, 153.
9. Piano Quartet, Op. 16 (arrangement of the following): *EE* 114; *KSS* 1012.
10. Piano Quintet, Op. 16: *EE* 200; *KSS* 1011.
11. Chamber Music for Wind Instruments, Op. 25, 71, 87, 103: *KSS* 1007; *Lea* 100.
12. Sextet for two violins, viola, cello and two horns, Op. 81b: *IMC*.
13. Sextet, Op. 81b and Septet for clarinet, horn, bassoon, violin, viola, cello and double bass, Op. 20: *KSS* 1004; *Lea* 154.

Playing Parts and Scores

14. String Trios, Op. 3, 8, 9, Nos. 1-3: *CE*, Series 7; *IMC*; *PE* 194.
15. String Quartets (complete): *CE*, Series 6; *PE* 195a/b/c (new revised edition by Andreas Moser).
16. *Quatuors pour 2 violons, alto et violoncelle.* Braunschweig: H. Litolff, No. 63.
17. String Quintets, Op. 4, 29, 104, 137: *CE*, Series 5; *PE* 1599; Munich: G. Henle Verlag, 1973.
18. Piano Trios, Op. 1, 11, 44, 70, 97, 121: *CE*, Series 11; *PE* 166a (I-II), 166b; Munich: G. Henle Verlag, 1964-1968, 3 volumes.
19. *Six Celebrated Trios for Violin, Cello & Piano.* New York: International Music Company, 1948.
20. Piano Trio, Op. 97 (Archduke): *PE* 7067.
21. Piano Quartet, Op. 16 (arrangement of the Piano Quintet): *CE*, Series 10; *PE* 294.
22. Quintet for piano, oboe, clarinet, bassoon and horn, Op. 16: *CE*, Series 10; *PE*; *IMC*; Munich: G. Henle Verlag, 1971.
23. Sextet for two violins, viola, cello and two horns, Op. 81b: *CE*, Series 5; *PE* L-192.
24. Sextet for two clarinets, two bassoons, two horns, Op. 71: London: Hinrichsen Edition, 1963, Hinrichsen No. 738; New York: International Music Company, 1950.
25. Septet for violin, viola, horn, clarinet, bassoon, cello and double bass, Op. 20: *CE*, Series 5; *PE* 2446; New York: International Music Company, 1948.
26. Octet for two oboes, two clarinets, two bassoons and two horns, Op. 103: *CE*, Series 8; Leipzig: Breitkopf & Härtel, 1966.
27. Three *Equali* for four trombones. Wiesbaden: Breitkopf & Härtel, 1896.
28. (*CE*) *Ludwig van Beethoven Werke*, 46 volumes. Leipzig: Breitkopf & Härtel, 1862-1888. (reprint: Ann Arbor: Edwards, 1949; New York: E. F. Kalmus, 1968, in 66 volumes)
29. *Complete String Quartets and Grosse Fuge.* New York: Dover Publications. (reprint: Breitkopf & Härtel)

OUTLINE V

FRANZ PETER SCHUBERT (1797 - 1828)

I. Life

1797 Born in Liechtental [Lichtenthal], now part of Vienna, January 31.

1803-1807 Was taught voice, piano, violin and harmony by his father, a humble school-master, and his brothers.

1808-1813 Admitted to the school of the Vienna court choir. Trained by Antonio Salieri and Josef Eybler. Became the leader of the school orchestra. Played viola in a chamber music group when at home. Began composing about 1811.

1813-1816 Became a teacher in his father's school to avoid military service. Continued to compose.

1817-1827 Left home, living with friends when financially destitute. His whole time was devoted to composing; wrote symphonies, overtures, piano sonatas, dramatic works, choral music, masses and hundreds of songs. Exploited by publishers, he realized little from his compositions, and only late in life did he receive public recognition.

1828 Died in Vienna, November 19.

II. Catalogue of Chamber Music

A. String Instruments
1. Fifteen string quartets
2. *Quartettsatz* (1820)
3. One string trio (1817) (violin, viola, cello)
4. One string quintet (1828) (2 violins, 1 viola, 2 cellos)

B. Piano with other instruments
1. One sonata (1817) (violin, piano)
2. Three sonatinas (1816) (violin, piano)
3. One sonata (1824) (*arpeggione* or cello, piano)
4. Two trios (piano, violin, cello)
5. One piano quintet (piano, violin, viola, cello, contra-bass)
6. One octet (2 violins, viola, cello, bass, clarinet, bassoon, horn)

C. Miscellaneous
1. Nocturne, Op. 148 (1812); Rondo Brilliant, Op. 70 (1826); *Phantasie* in C major, Op. 159 (1827), also known as Sonata No. 4 (all for violin, piano)
2. Introduction and Variations, Op. 160 (flute, piano)
3. Sonata movement in B-flat major (1812) (piano, violin, cello)
4. Trio in B-flat major (one movement) (violin, viola, cello)
5. Adagio and Rondo Concertante in F major (1816) (piano, violin, viola, cello)
6. *Eine kleine Trauermusik* (1813) (2 clarinets, 2 bassoons, contra-bassoon, 2 horns, 2 trombones)
7. Minuetto and Finale (1813) (2 oboes, 2 clarinets, 2 bassoons, 2 horns)
8. Quartet (1814) (flute, guitar, viola, cello)

D. Opus numbers bear no relation to the chronological order of composition, because so few works were published before Schubert's death. Quartets, Op. 125, Nos. 1 and 2 were composed not later than 1817. The Quartet in A minor, Opus 29, was written in 1824. Quartets are numbered in some editions in addition to having opus indications, but the numbering is not standard. The Quartets are best identified by key.

III. Chamber Music

A. Schubert wrote a comparatively small amount of chamber music considering his entire output, but it represents a considerable amount of his instrumental music. Some of his immature works, that other composers would have destroyed, remain. His treatment of the piano in chamber music formed the foundation for the chamber music with piano of Robert Schumann and Johannes Brahms.

B. Two periods of composition
  1. The early period includes the first eleven quartets, three sonatinas for violin and piano, a string trio and lesser known works.
    a. These works all show Schubert's great melodic gifts and gradual development in the skill with which he handled musical ideas and the instrumental expression of them.
    b. His early quartets show great deviations in the matter of form. They are uneven in quality, and many are overlong. Other weaknesses include too much use of the violins in octaves, much reiteration of the same figure in middle voices, extensive use of tremolo and many repeated notes in succession.
  2. The mature period in Schubert's chamber works was reached in 1820 with the *Quartettsatz* in C minor. The Quintet for piano and strings ("The Trout") of 1819 belongs between the two periods.
    a. Many of the weaknesses of the early chamber music disappeared. Schubert adopted a new way of handling the instruments of the quartet, and the form became more concise and the writing more independent.

C. Characteristics of style
  1. Melody was both his strength and weakness. He used the regular division of "song-period" constantly.
  2. Instruments were grouped in twos and played off against each other, harmonic groups against each other, or a harmonic group against a linear phrase.
  3. There was little use of polyphony or polyphonic devices. He preferred to invent a new melody, or to modulate freely to other keys rather than develop an idea.
  4. Alternating major and minor tonality is characteristic of Schubert's style.

IV. String Quartets (Early Period)

A. Six Quartets (1812-1813)
  1. These reveal interest in harmonic color and variety. Use of orchestral effects: tremolo, unison passages, widely spaced chordal writing. Long melodic lines made up of many lyric themes, dramatic climaxes and loose forms are characteristic of these quartets.
  2. Not included in the six quartets was an early quartet in G major (1814), written for flute, viola, cello, guitar.

B. Quartet No. 7 in E-flat major, Op. 125, No. 1 (1814) (*M* 1, p. 310)
  1. Allegro moderato in E-flat major (2/2); Scherzo, Prestissimo in E-flat major (3/4). Trio in C minor; Adagio in E-flat major (6/8); Allegro in E-flat major (2/4).
  2. The first movement has the first theme in the tonic, the second theme in the dominant, two subsidiary themes.
  3. The Scherzo and Adagio are somewhat in early Beethoven style. Brilliant Finale.

C. Quartet No. 8 in D major (1814)
  1. Allegro in D major (4/4); Andante con moto in G major (4/4); Menuetto in D major (3/4); Presto in D major (2/4).
  2. The first movement shows development in breadth and power, but the other three movements are experimental. All have typical Schubert melodies (five in the first seventy measures). He uses the characteristic device of two themes of equal importance, the second following the first immediately.

D. Quartet No. 9 in B-flat major, Op. 168 (1814) (*M* 1, p. 317)

1. Allegro ma non troppo in B-flat major (4/4); Andante sostenuto in G minor (3/4); Menuetto in E-flat major (3/4); Presto in B-flat major (3/4).
2. This quartet shows a marked advance over the Quartet in D major. The first movement is in clearly defined sections with contrasting melodies, modulations and rhythms.
3. The second movement is in lyric style based mostly on the repetition of ideas in various tonalities.
4. The Minuet is in Haydn style, with a typical Schubert Trio and much two-part writing in octaves.
5. The Presto, in modified sonata-form, is in Scherzo style. The material is based on the first theme; the second idea (D minor) is only a variant of the first theme.

E. Quartet No. 10 in G minor (1815)
1. Allegro con brio in G minor (4/4); Andantino in B-flat major (2/4); Menuetto in B-flat major (3/4); Allegro in G minor (2/4).
2. The first movement has two contrasting themes in the tonic and dominant. The Development of thirty-two measures uses the second theme. The principal subject occurs at the beginning of the Recapitulation in the relative major.
3. The second movement has the characteristic hesitation between major and minor, and unusual modulations.
4. The Finale is in a modified rondo form.

F. Quartet No. 11 in E major, Op. 125, No. 2 (1817)
1. Allegro con fuoco in E major (4/4); Andante in A major (2/4); Menuetto in E major (3/4); Rondeau: Allegro vivace in E major (2/4).
2. Less doubling of parts with more four-part writing. New uses of instrumental color.
3. The theme used near the beginning of the first movement becomes, in a varied form, the principal theme of the Finale.
4. The slow movement is exceedingly florid.
5. The Finale is in rondo form.

V. String Quartets (Mature Period)

A. *Quartettsatz* in C minor (1820) (*M* 1, p. 327)
1. Allegro assai (6/8). The first movement of an unfinished quartet.
2. The beginning of Schubert's mature period of chamber music composition. A new style of using instruments; each used independently; doubling of parts avoided.

B. Quartet No. 13 in A minor, Op. 29 (1824) (*M* 1, p. 270)
1. Allegro ma non troppo in A minor (4/4); Andante in C major (4/4); Menuetto in A minor (3/4); Allegro moderato in A major (2/4).
2. This is the only quartet published in Schubert's lifetime. Quiet, somber style and one of his finest works.
3. The principal subject of the slow movement is a melody used in *Rosamunde* ballet music, and the *Impromptu*, Op. 142, No. 3.
4. The Minuet uses a theme from his setting of Schiller's "Gods of Greece."
5. The Finale is in sonata-form. Strong rhythmic and melodic characteristics suggest Hungarian influence.

C. Quartet No. 14 in D minor ("Death and the Maiden") (1824) (*M* 1, p. 295)
1. Allegro in D minor (4/4); Andante con moto (theme and variations) in G minor (2/2); Scherzo: Allegro molto in D minor (3/4); Presto in D minor (6/8).
2. An outstanding work and the best known of the quartets.
3. The first movement has five main ideas, three in the tonic, two in the relative minor. A triplet figure plays an important part in the movement. The second theme (meas. 61) begins the Development (meas. 141). Recapitulation (meas. 198); Coda (meas. 299).
4. The Andante movement is a set of five variations and Coda based on the theme in the

accompaniment of the song "Death and the Maiden." The treatment of the theme is less free than with Beethoven; each variation portrays a different mood.

5. The Scherzo is vigorous and concise. Form: Scherzo (meas. 1-68) - Trio in D major (meas. 69-164) - Scherzo.

6. The Finale is a long, powerful movement in rondo form: A (meas. 1-88) - B (meas. 89-317) - A with short Development (meas. 318-446) - B (meas. 447-651) - A and Coda (meas. 652-754). The *Erlkönig* theme is introduced (meas. 134).

D. Quartet No. 15 in G major, Op. 161 (1826) (*M* 1, p. 280

1. Allegro molto moderato in G major (3/4); Andante un poco molto in E minor (4/4); Scherzo: Allegro vivace in B minor (3/4); Allegro assai in G major (6/8).

2. Schubert's last quartet. It uses many orchestral effects, with emphasis on shifting harmonies, rather than melodic lines. Characteristic alternation of major and minor is found in the first and last movements.

VI. Two Quintets

A. Quintet in A major, Op. 114 ("The Trout") (1819) (*M* 1, p. 212)

1. Allegro vivace in A major (4/4); Andante in F major (3/4); Scherzo: Presto in A major (3/4); Andantino: Theme and Variations in D major (2/4); Finale: Allegro giusto in A major (2/4).

2. Instrumentation: piano, violin, viola, cello, contra-bass. The first work in which Schubert used one of his songs as the subject for variations. (Quartet No. 14 is dated 1824.) The work is unusual in the use of the string bass. This is the first composition by any major composer for piano and four strings, but not strictly speaking a piano quintet as the usual string quartet combination is not used. Quintets by Mozart and Beethoven are for piano and wind instruments.

3. The first movement is in sonata-form; the second theme (meas. 54) is given to the cello. The Development begins in measure 147; Recapitulation in measure 210.

4. The second movement is in three contrasting sections (F major, F-sharp minor and D major, ending in G major) which are repeated a minor third higher in A-flat major, A minor and F major.

5. The third movement is a Scherzo (meas. 1-104) and Trio (meas. 105-170).

6. The fourth movement is a theme and six variations on "The Trout." The sixth variation has the piano accompaniment from the song.

7. The fifth movement is an Allegro giusto in A major which has a Hungarian rhythm. It is in sonata-form without a Development section and with a Recapitulation (meas. 237) which is an exact transposition of the Exposition up a fifth. The second theme in the Exposition begins in measure 84.

B. Quintet in C major, Op. 163 (1828) (*M* 1, p. 192)

1. Allegro ma non troppo in C major (4/4); Adagio in E major (12/8); Scherzo: Presto in C major (3/4); Allegretto in C major (2/2).

2. Instrumentation: 2 violins, viola, 2 cellos. It is generally considered to be Schubert's finest chamber work. The use of a second cello gives the first cello greater melodic freedom.

3. The first movement uses two lyric themes and subsidiary melodies. There is greater variety in the use of the instruments.

4. The second movement is in three contrasting sections in E major, F minor, E major.

5. The Scherzo (3/4) is in strongly contrasting moods and meters. The Trio (4/4) is an Andante sostenuto in D-flat major.

6. The Finale begins in C minor, but is in C major from measure 19. The tempo increases at the end to Più allegro, concluding with a Più presto.

VII. Two Piano Trios

A. Trio in B flat. Op. 99 (1827) (piano, violin, cello) (*M* 1, p. 235)
  1. Allegro moderato in B-flat major (4/4); Andante un poco mosso in E-flat major (6/8); Scherzo in B-flat major (3/4); Rondo in B-flat major (2/4).
  2 Written for a trio composed of Ignaz Schuppanzigh and Joseph Lincke (friends of Beethoven and members of the Razumovsky Quartet) and the pianist Karl von Bocklet. The two trios represent Schubert at his best.
  3. The first movement is in Sonata-form. It is built on two contrasting themes and fragments, which are repeated with different harmonic effects.
  4. The second movement is in three sections.
  5. The Finale is a movement of great length in Rondo form. It is based on a folk-like melody.

B. Trio in E-flat major, Op. 100 (1827) (piano, violin, cello) (*M* 1, p. 251)
  1. Allegro in E-flat major (3/4); Andante con moto in C minor (2/4); Scherzo: Allegro moderato in E-flat major (3/4); Allegro moderato in E-flat major (6/8).
  2. The first movement has many changes of tonality and signature. The characteristic accompaniment figure of the first movement reappears in the last movement, an unusual device for Schubert.
  3. The second movement is in the form of a March.
  4. The third movement is based on a canon between the piano and strings in octaves. The second part of the movement is based on a modified inversion of the canon theme.
  5. The Finale is the longest of the four long movements. It is in the typical Schubert sonata-form. The principal subject of the slow movement (meas. 275, 693), is introduced, but in the tempo and rhythm of the Finale. The second theme (meas. 73) is modified (meas. 125) and developed (meas. 163). Development (meas. 315); Recapitulation (meas. 441), second theme is in F minor (meas. 559).

SELECTED BIBLIOGRAPHY

Books

1. Abraham, Gerald. *Schubert, A Symposium*. New York: W. W. Norton, 1947. (Chamber Music: pp. 88-110)
2. Antcliffe, Herbert. *Schubert*. London: G. Bell and Sons, 1910.
3. Bie, Oscar. *Schubert, the Man*, tr. Jean Starr Untermeyer. New York: Dodd, Mead & Co., 1928. (Chamber Music: pp. 123-153)
4. Brent-Smith, Alexander. *Schubert—Quartet in D minor and Octet*. New York: Oxford University Press, 1927.
5. Brown, Maurice J. *Essays on Schubert*. New York: St. Martin's Press, 1966.
6. ——————*Schubert; a Critical Biography*. New York: St. Martin's Press, 1958.
7. Deutsch, Otto Erich. *Franz Schubert Thematisches Verzeichnis seiner Werke in chronologischer Folge*. Kassel: Bärenreiter, 1978.
8. ——————*Franz Schubert's Letters and Other Writings*, tr. Venetia Savile. New York: Alfred A. Knopf, 1928.
9. ——————*Schubert—A Documentary Biography*, tr. Eric Blom. New York: Da Capo Press, 1977.
10. ——————*Schubert: Memoirs by His Friends*, tr. Rosamond Ley and John Nowell. New York: Macmillan, 1958.
11. ——————*The Schubert Reader*, tr. Eric Blom. New York: W. W. Norton, 1947.
12. ——————*Schubert Thematic Catalogue of All His Works in Chronological Order*. New York: W. W. Norton, 1951.
13. Duncan, Edmondstoune. *Schubert*. New York: E. P. Dutton and Co., 1934.

14. Einstein, Alfred. *Schubert; a Musical Portrait*. New York: Oxford University Press, 1951.
15. Flower, Newman. *Franz Schubert, the Man and His Circle*. London: Cassell, 1949.
16. Humiston, William Henry. *Schubert*. New York: Breitkopf Publications, 1925.
17. Hutchings, Arthur. *Schubert*, 3rd ed. London: J. M. Dent, 1956; New York: Farrar, Straus and Cudahy, 1956.
18. Kobald, Karl. *Franz Schubert and His Times*, tr. Beatrice Marshall. New York: Alfred A. Knopf, 1928.
19. Mason, Daniel Gregory. *The Romantic Composers*. New York: Macmillan, 1926.
20. Reed, John. *Schubert*. London: Faber & Faber, 1978.
21. –––––––*Schubert, the Final Years*. London: Faber & Faber, 1972.
22. Schauffler, Robert H. *Franz Schubert: the Ariel of Music*. New York: G. P. Putnam, 1949.
23. Wechsberg, Joseph. *Schubert: His Life, His Work, His Time*. New York: Rizzoli International Publications, 1977.
24. Wells-Harrison, W. *Schubert's Compositions for Piano and Strings*. New York: Scribner, 1915.
25. Whitaker, Wilson Cecil. *Franz Schubert, Man and Composer*. London: W. Reeves, 1928.

Articles

1. Adler, Guido. "Schubert and the Viennese Classical School," tr. Theodore Baker. *MQ* 14 (1928), pp. 273-285.
2. Beechey, Gwilym E. "Rhythmic Interpretation; Mozart, Beethoven, Schubert and Schumann." *MR* 33 (1972), pp. 233-248.
3. Boughton, R. "Schubert and Melodic Design." *MT* 69 (1928), p. 881.
4. Brown, Maurice J. "Small Latin and Less Counterpoint." *MR* 8 (1947), pp. 175-177.
5. –––––––"Schubert and Neapolitan Relationships." *MT* 85 (1944), p. 43.
6. Bruce, Robert. "The Lyrical Element in Schubert's Instrumental Forms." *MR* 30 (1969), pp. 131-137.
7. Capell, Richard. "Schubert's Style." *MT* 69 (1928), p. 304.
8. Coolidge, Richard A. "Form in the String Quartets of Franz Schubert." *MR* 32 (1971), pp. 309-325.
9. Dale, Kathleen. "Schubert's Indebtedness to Haydn." *ML* 21 (1940), pp. 23-30.
10. Dent, Edward J. "The Style of Schubert." *Dominant* 1, No. 8 (Jun 1928).
11. Deutsch, Otto Erich. "The Chronology of Schubert's String Quartets." *ML* 24 (1943), pp. 25-30).
12. Eibner, Franz. "The Dotted-Quaver-and-Semiquaver Figure with Triplet Accompaniment in the Works of Schubert." *MR* 23 (1962), pp. 281-284.
13. Engel, Carl. "Schubert's Fame." *MQ* 14 (1928), pp. 457-472.
14. Költzsch, Hans. "Schubert and the Romantic Problem." *ML* 20 (1939), pp. 130-137.
15. Laciar, Samuel L. "The Chamber-Music of Franz Schubert." *MQ* 14 (1928), pp. 515-538.
16. Mann, B. P. "Schubert's String Quartet in A minor." *Strad* 65 (Dec 1954), p. 256.
17. Newman, William S. "Freedom of Tempo in Schubert's Instrumental Music." *MQ* 61 (1975), pp. 528-545.
18. Rawlinson, Harold. "The Schubert Sonatinas." *Strad* 68 (Sept 1957), p. 166.
19. Smith, Alexander Brent. "Franz Schubert." *New Mus Rev* 30 (1931), p. 425.
20. "Franz Schubert." special issue, *Mus Courier* (April 12, 1928).
21. Truscott, Harold. "Schubert's D minor Quartet [Death and the Maiden]." *MR* 19 (1958), pp. 27-36.
22. –––––––"Schubert's String Quartet in G major." *MR* 20 (1959), pp. 119-145.
23. Webster, James C. "Schubert's Sonata Form and Brahm's First Maturity." *Nineteenth Century Music* 2, No. 1 (1978), pp. 18-35.
24. Weiss, Piero. "Dating the 'Trout' Quartet." *JAMS* 32 (1979), pp. 539-548.

SALEM COLLEGE SCHOOL OF MUSIC

25. Whaples, Mariam K. "On Structural Integration in Schubert's Instrumental Works." *Acta Mus* 40, Nos. 2-3 (1968), pp. 186-195.

Music

Study (Miniature) Scores

1. *The Chamber Music of Haydn and Schubert*, ed. Albert E. Wier. Melville, NY: Belwin-Mills, 1973.
2. String Quartets: *EE* 11, 39, 40, 116, 117, 119, 120, 353, 354; *KSS* 788, 789, 790; *Lea* 51, 52, 53; *Ph* 350-355.
3. String Quartet in A minor, Op. 29: *BH* 186.
4. String Quartet in G major, Op. 161: *BH* 187.
5. String Quintet in C major, Op. 163: *EE* 15; *KSS* 791.
6. Piano Trios: *EE* 84, 85; *KSS*; *Lea* 110; *Ph* 369.
7. Piano Quintet in A major, Op. 114 (The Trout): *BH* 185; *EE* 118; *KSS* 791; *Lea* 111; *Ph* 375.
8. Octet in F major, Op. 166: *EE* 60; *KSS* 1034; *Lea* 156.

Playing Parts and Scores

9. Trio No. 2 in B-flat major for violin, viola, cello: New York: International Music Company.
10. String Quartets, Op. 29, 125, 161, 168: *CE*, Series 5; *DV*, v. 2; *PE* 168a/b.
11. String Quintet in C major, Op. 163: *CE*, Series 4; *DV*, v. 2; *PE* 775.
12. Octet in F, Op. 166: *CE*, Series 3; *DV*, v. 2; *PE* 1849; New York: International Music Company, 1948.
13. Piano Trios, Op. 99, 100: *CE*, Series 7; *DV*. v. 3; *PE* 167; Munich: G. Henle Verlag, 1973.
14. Piano Quintet in A major, Op. 114 (The Trout): *CE*, Series 7; *DV* v. 3; *PE* 169; New York: International Music Company, 1943.
15. (*CE*) *Schubert Gesamtausgabe*, 21 Series in 39 volumes. Leipzig: Brietkopf & Härtel, 1883-1895. (reprint: New York: E. F. Kalmus in 97 volumes; [*DV*] New York: Dover Publications,1964, in 19 volumes)
16. *Complete Chamber Music for Pianoforte and Strings*. New York: Dover Publications. (reprint: Breitkopf & Härtel)
17. *Complete Chamber Music for Strings*. New York: Dover Publications. (reprint: Breitkopf & Härtel)

OUTLINE VI

JACOB LUDWIG FELIX MENDELSSOHN (1809 - 1847)

I. Life

1809	Born in Hamburg, February 4, into a wealthy and cultured family. Moved to Berlin in 1812. The name Bartholdy was added to Mendelssohn when the family became Protestants.
1816	Studied with Ludwig Berger, Carl Friedrich Zelter, Henning, the violinist, Mme. Marie Bigot in Paris, and Ignaz Moscheles (1824). Met famous artists, writers, and other distinguished people at his home.
1820	Began to compose at the age of eleven. By 1825 he was an accomplished pianist, organist, violinist and composer. His Overture to "A Midsummer Night's Dream" was written in 1825 at the age of sixteen.
1829	Directed the Singakademie in a performance of Bach's "St. Matthew Passion" (1829), the first since Bach's death. Traveled in England, Italy, Switzerland and France. Declined the offer of a position at the University of Berlin.
1833	Became music director at Düsseldorf (1833-1835); conductor of the Gewandhaus Orchestra in Leipzig (1835). Made many trips, especially to England. Friendship with Robert Schumann.
1837	Married Cécile Jeanrenaud, daughter of a Swiss clergyman. Received an honorary Doctor of Philosophy degree from the University of Leipzig.
1843	Organized the Conservatory of Leipzig, which had a distinguished faculty, including Schumann. Music director at the courts in Berlin and Dresden; continued conducting and traveling.
1847	Died in Leipzig, November 4, at the age of thirty-eight.

II. Catalogue of Chamber Music

A. Six String Quartets and four Quartet movements
B. Two String Quintets (2 violins, 2 violas, cello)
C. String Octet in E-flat major, Op. 20 (4 violins, 2 violas, 2 cellos)
D. Three Sonatas with Piano
  1. Sonata for Violin and Piano, Op. 14 in F minor
  2. Two sonatas for Cello and Piano
    a. Op. 45 in B-flat major; Op. 58 in D major
E. Trios with Piano
  1. Op. 49 in D minor; Op. 66 in C minor (piano, violin, cello)
  2. Two Pieces, Op. 113 in F major; Op. 114 in D minor (piano, clarinet, basset-horn)
F. Three Piano Quartets
  1. Op. 1 in C minor; Op. 2 in F minor; Op. 3 in B minor
G. Sextet, Op. 110 in D major (piano, violin, 2 violas, cello, contra-bass)

III. Chamber Music

A. Mendelssohn's first chamber music (Piano Quartets, Op. 1, 2, 3) was written before the age of fifteen.
  1. His style was based on a natural sense of form and good taste. His music is correct, suave, polished, and his melodies are facile and charming, but rarely intense.
  2. He was especially successful in Scherzo movements and developed a new type in duple

meter in large rondo form. The old minuet-scherzo with trio disappeared.

3.   A conservative Romanticist as regards form, he generally followed existing paths.

IV.   String Quartets

A.   Op. 13 in A minor (1827)
1.   Unusual in the use of his song "Is it true?" (Op. 9, No. 1) at the beginning and end. The second theme of the first movement is used in the Finale (cyclic). The Recitative is used in the slow movement.
B.   Op. 12 in E-flat major (1829)
1.   This shows characteristics of his mature style, although it was written at the age of twenty. The introduction suggests Beethoven's Op. 74 ("Harp" quartet). The second theme is related rhythmically to the first. The mood is lyric throughout.
2.   The "Canzonetta" takes the place of a Scherzo. It makes effective use of pizzicato and staccato, with a humorous conclusion.
3.   The Finale uses themes from the first movement (cyclic).
C.   Three String Quartets, Op. 44 (1837-1838)
1.   Op. 44, No. 1 in D major
a.   The brilliant first and last movements are in orchestral style. A melodious Minuet and an Andantino in "song-without-words" style complete the work.
2.   Op. 44, No. 2 in E minor
a.   A remarkable elfin-like Scherzo. The Finale is in rondo form with the principal theme in country-dance style.
3.   Op. 44, No. 3 in E-flat major
a.   An outstanding quartet. It includes fugal sections, imitations, clear forms, striking themes, lyrical melodies and a sparkling Scherzo.
D.   Op. 80 in F minor (1847)
1.   This was written nine years after Op. 44, possibly inspired by the death of his sister Fanny. A solemn work, somewhat inferior to the other quartets.
E.   Quartet movements, Op. 81
1.   Andante in E major (1847); Scherzo in A minor (1847); Capriccio in E minor (1843); Fugue in E-flat major (1847). Published in 1850 as Op. 81.

V.   Two String Quintets (2 violins, 2 violas, cello)

A.   Op. 18 in A major (1826, rewritten in 1832)
1.   Not a distinguished work, although the Scherzo with its fugato treatment of the main theme is typically Mendelssohn.
B.   Op. 87 in B-flat major (1845)
1.   The only outstanding movement is the Adagio. There is much use of orchestral tremolos, and the themes are generally undistinguished.

VI.   String Octet, Op. 20 in E-flat major (1825) (4 violins, 2 violas, 2 cellos)

A.   This is the first string octet which treats the two quartets as an eight-voiced work (in Louis Spohr's octets, the second quartet plays an accompanying or antiphonal part). All instruments take part in the ensemble, although the brilliant first violin sometimes dominates. There are many orchestral effects. Mendelssohn said the work should be played in symphonic style.
B.   The first movement opens with a vigorous theme (1st violin) accompanied by tremolo and syncopations. A fanfare motive enters in measure 21 and a quiet second theme in measure 68. The Recapitulation varies the material somewhat, and the Coda begins with a fanfare motive.

C. The Scherzo is staccato and soft throughout; the outstanding movement of the Octet. Later Mendelssohn arranged this for orchestra.

D. The Finale begins with a fugal exposition and the Scherzo movement reappears.

VII. **Two Trios for Piano, Violin, Cello**

A. Op. 49 in D minor (1839) (*M* 1, p. 195)
   1. The Trios are among Mendelssohn's best chamber works. Perfection of form and detail is everywhere in evidence. Schumann considered Op. 49 comparable to Beethoven's B-flat major and D major Trios and Schubert's in E-flat major.
   2. The Scherzo, as usual, and the Andante con moto are outstanding movements.

B. Op. 66 in C minor (1845)
   1. The Allegro energico begins with a strong theme emphasizing the key of C minor, followed by a contrasting expressive second theme. One of his finest movements.
   2. The melodious Andante espressivo is followed by a virtuoso Scherzo.
   3. The Finale is another masterpiece. The agitated principal theme begins with the interval of a ninth. The contrasting second theme is not much used. The Coda in C major uses the first theme.

VIII. **Sextet in D major, Op. 110 (1824) (piano, violin, 2 violas, cello, contra-bass)**

A. An experimental early work of little merit. It shows, however, Mendelssohn's gift for clear form. The Minuet, in unusual 6/8 time, appears in the Finale before the Coda.

SELECTED BIBLIOGRAPHY

Books

1. Benedict, Sir Julius. *Sketch of the Life and Works of the Late Felix Mendelssohn-Bartholdy,* 2nd ed. London: G. F. Murray, 1853.
2. Hensel, Sebastian. *The Mendelssohn Family,* 2 volumes, 2nd rev. ed., tr. Carl Klingemann. New York: Greenwood Press, 1968. (reprint: New York: Harper & Brothers, 1882)
3. Hurd, Michael. *Mendelssohn.* London: Faber & Faber, 1970.
4. Jacob, Heinrich Eduard. *Felix Mendelssohn and His Time,* tr. Richard and Clara Winston. Englewood Cliffs, NJ: Prentice-Hall, 1963.
5. Kaufman, Schima. *Mendelssohn, a Second Elijah.* New York: T. Y. Crowell Co., 1934.
6. Kupferberg, Herbert. *Felix Mendelssohn: His Life, His Family, His Music.* New York: Charles Scribner's, 1972.
7. Lampadius, Wilhelm Adolf. *The Life of Felix Mendelssohn-Bartholdy,* tr. William Leonhard Gage. New York: H. Ditson and Co., 1887.
8. Marek, Georg R. *Gentle Genius; the Story of Felix Mendelssohn.* New York: Funk and Wagnalls, 1972.
9. Radcliffe, Philip. *Mendelssohn.* London: J. M. Dent, 1967; New York: Farrar, Straus and Giroux, 1967.
10. Rockstro, William Smyth. *Mendelssohn.* London: S. Low, Marston & Co., 1884.
11. Selden-Goth, Gisella, ed. *Letters of Felix Mendelssohn-Bartholdy.* New York: Pantheon, 1945.
12. Stratton, Stephen S. *Mendelssohn.* New York: E. P. Dutton, 1934.
13. *Thematisches Verzeichnis der im Druck erschienenen Compositionen von Felix Mendelssohn-Bartholdy.* Leipzig: Breitkopf & Härtel, 1878.
14. Werner, Eric. *Mendelssohn: A New Image of the Composer and His Age,* tr. Dika Newlin. New York: Free Press, 1963.

Articles

1. Foss, Hubert J. "A Commentary upon Mendelssohn." *MT* 65 (1924), p. 404.
2. Ricker, Charles. "Review of Mendelssohn's Letters." *Kenyon Rev* 7 (1945), p. 728.
3. Smith, Alexander B. "The Workmanship of Mendelssohn." *ML* 4 (1923), pp. 18-25.
4. Watson, Sara Ruth. "Mendelssohn: The First Maestro." *Mus Am* 67 (Sept 1947), p. 5.
5. Whittaker, William Gillies. "Mendelssohn's Octet." *MT* 74 (1933), p. 322.

Music

Study (Miniature) Scores

1. *Miscellaneous Chamber Works*, ed. Albert E. Wier. Melville, NY: Belwin-Mills, 1973.
2. String Quartets: *EE* 7, 47, 48, 49, 68, 101, 102; *KSS* 1184, 1185; *Lea* 149, 150; *Ph* 348, 349.
3. String Quintet, Op. 18: *EE* 134; *KSS* 1183; *Lea* 148.
4. String Quintet, Op. 87: *EE* 67; *KSS* 184; *Lea* 148.
5. String Octet, Op. 20: *KSS* 1182; *Lea* 148.
6. Piano Trios, Op. 49, 66: *EE* 80, 81.

Playing Parts and Scores

7. String Quartets, Op. 12, 13, 44, 80, 81: *CE*, Series 6; *PE* 1742.
8. *4 Celebrated Quartets*, Op. 12, 44, Nos. 1, 2, 3. New York: International Music Company.
9. String Quintets, Op. 18, 87: *CE*, Series 5; *PE* 1743.
10. String Octet, Op. 20: *CE*, Series 5; *PE* 1782.
11. Piano Trios, Op. 49, 66: *CE*, Series 9; *PE* 1740.
12. Piano Trios, Op. 49, 66. Munich: G. Henle Verlag, 1972.
13. Piano Quartets, Op. 1, 2, 3: *CE*, Series 9; *PE* 1741.
14. Piano Sextet, Op. 110: *CE*, Series 9; *Litolff* 636.
15. (*CE*) *Felix Mendelssohn-Bartholdy Werke*, ed. Julius Rietz, 19 Series in 37 volumes. Leipzig: Breitkopf & Härtel, 1874-1877. (reprint: Farnborough, Hantshire, England: Gregg Press, 1977; New York: E. F. Kalmus, in 61 volumes)
16. Felix Mendelssohn. *Complete Chamber Music for Strings*. New York: Dover Publications, 1978. (reprint: Leipzig: Breitkopf & Härtel)

OUTLINE VII

ROBERT ALEXANDER SCHUMANN (1810 - 1856)

I. Life

1810   Born in Zwickau, Saxony, June 8. His father was a book seller and publisher.

1825   Became attracted by the fantastic, sentimental, romantic writings of Jean Paul (Johann Paul Friedrich Richter).

1828   Sent to the University of Leipzig to study law and in 1829 to the University of Heidelberg. Continued the study of piano.

1830   Left the University to study piano with Friedrich Wieck; injured his hand with a mechanical device and turned to composition. Wrote only piano music up to 1839.

1834   Founded the *Neue Zeitschrift für Musik*, which he edited until 1844. This journal exerted a wide influence on the musical life and taste of the time. Began his friendship with Felix Mendelssohn.

1838   Visited Vienna and recovered many Franz Schubert manuscripts.

1840   Married Clara Wieck. Composed many songs, orchestral compositions (1841), chamber music (1843). Often went on tours with his wife, an excellent pianist.

1843   Became a member of the faculty of the new Leipzig Conservatory. Ill health prompted a move to Dresden in 1844.

1850   Followed Ferdinand Hiller as municipal music director at Düsseldorf, but was not a success as a conductor. Continued composing.

1853   Forced to retire because of a mental breakdown. Meeting with Johannes Brahms.

1854   Attempted to take his own life by drowning in the Rhine. He spent his remaining days in a sanatorium in a state of mental derangement.

1856   Died July 29 near Bonn.

II. Catalogue of Chamber Music

A. Three String Quartets, Op. 41, No. 1 in A minor; No. 2 in F major; No. 3 in A major (1842) Dedicated to Mendelssohn.

B. Piano Quintet in E-flat major, Op. 44 (1842)

C. Piano Quartet in E-flat major, Op. 47 (1842)

D. Trios for Piano, Violin, Cello
  1. Trio in D minor, Op. 63 (1847)
  2. Trio in F major, Op. 80 (1847)
  3. Trio in G minor, Op. 110 (1851)
  4. *Fantasiestücke*, Op. 88 (1842) (character pieces like *Papillon, Kreisleriana*)

E. Sonatas for Piano, Violin
  1. Sonata in A minor, Op. 105 (1851)
  2. Sonata in D minor, Op. 121 (1851)

F. Miscellaneous
  1. *Märchenbilder* Suite (piano, viola), Op. 113 (1851)
  2. *Fantasiestücke* (piano, clarinet), Op. 73 (1849)
  3. *Märchenerzählungen* (piano, clarinet, viola), Op. 132 (1853)
  4. Adagio and Allegro (piano, horn), Op. 70 (1849)
  5. Three Romances (piano, oboe), Op. 94 (1849)
  6. Five *Stücke im Volkston* (piano, cello), Op. 102 (1849)

SALEM COLLEGE SCHOOL OF MUSIC

III. Chamber Music

A. Schumann's first and greatest chamber music was composed in 1842. He studied the string quartets of Franz Joseph Haydn and Wolfgang Amadeus Mozart and sought advice of Mendelssohn, Joseph Joachim and Ferdinand David. He was generally most successful in small forms and mood pieces.

B. Characteristics of his style are sudden changes of mood, a tendency to write in pianistic style for string instruments, use of minor keys (especially A and D), dotted rhythms, rising and falling scale lines, falling minor third returning a half step upward, falling fifths, lyric unity, melodic doubling, basic sonority of open octaves, standard key relationships, sudden dynamic contrasts and rhythmic accents on weak beats.

C. Romantic characteristics appear frequently in the quiet, expressive melodies. Schumann was frequently unable, in his chamber music, to sustain a high level of inspiration. He was unable to give up classicism entirely, or to give himself up completely to romanticism.

IV. String Quartets, Op. 41, dedicated to Mendelssohn

A. Op. 41, No. 1 in A minor (1842) (*M* 1, p. 232)
  1. Introduzione, Andante expressivo (A minor) - Allegro (F major)
    a. The introduction is based on imitation and modulates to F for the Allegro. The principal theme contains material for the whole movement.
    b. The first section (meas. 34-75) is based on a theme in two parts. The second section begins in measure 56 with characteristic accents in the second half of the measure. A new theme (meas. 76) is treated in a short fugato followed by a second fugato, which is an extension of the second part of the first theme (meas. 99-136).
    c. The Development (meas. 151-252) uses material already presented, with great freedom and interesting modulations. The Recapitulation (meas. 253-355) is followed by a Coda (meas. 365-374).
  2. Scherzo (A minor)
    a. There are three sections: Scherzo in 6/8 (meas. 1-82); Intermezzo in *Alla Breve* (meas. 83-115); Recapitulation of Scherzo (meas. 27). The use of a germ rhythm recalls Beethoven. The Intermezzo in place of a Trio shows an effort to change the classic forms. The Scherzo is often the second movement.
  3. Adagio (F major)
    a. This is a three-part form with the use of the variation principle: Introduction (meas. 1-3); Part I (meas. 4-28); Part II, free variation of Part I (meas. 29-43); Part III, varied recapitulation of Part I (meas. 44-62); the Coda uses Introductory figures (meas. 63-67).
    b. Part I includes: first theme (meas. 4), second theme (meas. 16), varied recapitulation of the first theme (meas. 20-27), modulation to A-flat major for Part II (meas. 28). Sudden contrast of mood in the middle section is a characteristic of Schumann's style.
  4. Presto (A minor - A major)
    a. Sonata-form: Exposition (meas. 1-80); Development (meas. 81-209); expanded Recapitulation (meas. 210-289); Coda (meas. 290-324). The key of F appears in the Development, returning to A minor for the Recapitulation and to A major for the Coda.
    b. The basic material of the movement consists of ascending broken thirds derived from the first theme. A subsidiary theme (meas. 43) introduces a contrasting descending scale line. Another subsidiary theme enters (meas. 63) which is used in the Development with the first interval inverted. "Musette" in A major (meas. 258) is followed by the Coda (meas. 290), which uses broken third and descending scale

themes. The first theme does not appear.
B. Op. 41, No. 2 in F major
   1. Allegro vivace (F major)
     a. Sonata-form with material derived from the first theme. Exposition (meas. 1-96); Development (meas. 97-181); Recapitulation (meas. 182-261); Coda (meas. 261-281). The secondary theme (meas. 68) and closing theme (meas. 80) are an extension of the smooth-flowing romantic principal theme.
   2. Andante, quasi Variazioni (A-flat major)
     a. Variations in rhapsodic style in three parts
       1) Part I: Principal theme (meas. 1-8) followed by a secondary subject (meas. 8-16), possibly a variation of the principal theme, and an altered version (meas. 16-32) of the principal section.
       2) Part II: First variation (meas. 32-48); second (meas. 48-64); third (meas. 64-76); fourth (meas. 76-89).
       3) Part III (meas. 89-105) is a shortened recapitulation of Part I; Coda (meas. 105-112).
   3. Scherzo: Presto (C minor)
     a. Scherzo (meas. 1-88); Trio (meas. 89-122); Scherzo (meas. 122-170); Coda (meas. 171-195).
     b. A brilliant, difficult movement with a Trio in the style of Mendelssohn.
   4. Allegro molto vivace (F major)
     a. Sonata-form: Exposition (meas. 1-50); Development (meas. 51-152); Recapitulation (meas. 153-195); Coda (meas. 195-227).
     b. There is a strong resemblance to the finale of his "Spring Symphony," Op. 38 (1841) in principal themes and ascending scales (meas. 28-35). The movement makes much use of jagged imitations.
C. Op. 41, No. 3 in A major (1842) (*M* 1, p. 244)
   1. Andante expressivo - Allegro molto moderato (A major)
     a. Sonata-form: Introduction (meas. 1-7); Exposition (meas. 8-101); Development (meas. 102-145); shortened Recapitulation (meas. 146-209); Coda (meas. 210-226).
     b. The falling interval of a perfect fifth is used in various ways. Off-beat accompaniment passages suggest pianistic style.
   2. Assai agitato (F minor)
     a. Variations with the theme appearing after the third variation. Variation I (meas. 1-45); Variation II (meas. 49-96); Variation III, *L'istesso tempo* (meas. 97-144); Theme, *un poco Adagio* (meas. 145-192); Variation IV (meas. 192-224); Coda (meas. 224-255).
     b. There is a variety of mood, with the usual variation types avoided. The type of variation is that used by Sibelius.
   3. Adagio molto (D major)
     a. Three-part form: Part I (meas. 1-44); Part II (meas. 44-77); Part III (meas. 77-94); Coda (meas. 94-105).
     b. The first theme appears in measures 1, 44, 77; the second theme in measures 19, 58, 94 (suggested).
   4. Allegro molto vivace (A major)
     a. Rondo combined with large ternary form
       1) Part I: main theme (meas. 1); first subordinate theme (meas. 14); main theme (meas. 34); second subordinate theme (meas. 48); main theme (meas. 64); third subordinate theme (meas. 72).
       2) Part II: main theme (meas. 112); first subordinate theme (meas. 126); main theme (meas. 146); second subordinate theme (meas. 160); main theme (meas. 176); third subordinate theme (meas. 184).
       3) Part III: main theme, Coda (meas. 224).

b.   The main theme is in dotted-note rhythm (used in the third movement) and appears seven times. There are three subordinate themes, each appearing twice.

V.   Piano and Strings

A.   Quintet for Piano and Strings in E-flat major, Op. 44 (1843) (*M* 1, p. 254)
 1.   This is the first piano quintet with piano and string quartet. The second Trio of the second movement was revised at Mendelssohn's suggestion. The piano balances the four strings and often introduces themes. It plays almost continuously with only six measures rest in the entire work. The accompaniment figures are often broken chords; arpeggiated chords are rare. There is much use of full chords, often five-part with any note doubled. The piano often doubles strings for greater sonority.
 2.   Allegro brilliante (E-flat major)
    a.   Sonata-form: the first theme passes through several keys; the second theme is introduced by the piano (meas. 51) and stated by the cello (meas. 57); the codetta (meas. 108) uses part of the first theme in the dominant.
    b.   The Development begins with the establishment of the key of A-flat minor. The first theme is then introduced (meas. 1-28); the piano treats measures 3 and 4 of the first theme in diminution; modulations from A-flat minor through E-flat minor, B-flat minor, F minor and C minor. The first theme is in F minor (meas. 168) followed by modulations through G-flat minor, D-flat minor, A-flat minor, E-flat minor and finally through a chromatic line to the dominant of E-flat major.
    c.   The Recapitulation (meas. 207) repeats material of the Exposition almost exactly with the second theme in the tonic.
 3.   In modo d'una Marcia (C minor)
    a.   The melody with falling fifths is stated in the first violin, second violin and viola. The second section in C major (meas. 29-61), with the melody in the first violin, has an unusual rhythmic accompaniment in the piano and lower strings; the cello joins the melody in measure 53.
    b.   The return of the first theme is followed by an Agitato section in F minor; strong accents on the second beat of the theme; the first theme appears briefly with the triplet figure and tremolo accompaniment. The second theme returns in F major (meas. 133) and the first theme in C minor (meas. 165).
 4.   Scherzo molto vivace (E-flat major)
    a.   The Scherzo is based on ascending and some descending scale passages. Form: Scherzo (meas. 1-45); Trio I (meas. 45-76); Scherzo (meas. 76-121); Trio II (meas. 122-195); Scherzo (meas. 196-239); Coda (meas. 239-264).
    b.   The Trio I (G-flat major) has the characteristic falling fifth. The theme is in canon with the viola. Trio II (A-flat minor) makes use of the characteristic shift in accent. A short section in E major returning to A-flat minor; ascending scale passages through all instruments; Coda (meas. 240).
 5.   Allegro, ma non troppo (C minor - E-flat major)
    a.   One of Schumann's best movements. Unusual skill is shown in the handling of contrapuntal material and in melodic invention.
    b.   Sonata-form with an unusual feature of two Expositions, two Developments, and two Recapitulations.
        1)   Exposition: first theme in C minor (meas. 1-42); second theme in G major (meas. 43-77); closing section in B minor (meas. 77-96). The Development (meas. 96-136) uses the first and second themes. The Recapitulation: first theme in C-sharp minor (meas. 136-178); second theme in E-flat major (meas. 178-212); closing section in G minor (meas. 212-224).
        2)   Exposition of the third theme in E-flat major (meas. 224-248); Development using parts of the first theme and a theme from the first movement (meas. 248-

378); Recapitulation of the third theme in E-flat major (meas. 378-402); The Coda is based on the first theme (meas. 402-427).

    c.   At measure 319 in the Development, the first themes of the last and first movements are used in a double fugue. This is an early use of the device of bringing back material from earlier movements in the last movement (cyclic idea).

B.   Quartet for Piano and Strings in E-flat major, Op. 47 (1843) (*M* 1, p. 275)

    1.   This follows the idea of his piano quintet. The Piano Quartet, however, is less brilliant; themes are often given to instruments in a weak register; the lower register is frequently used; the piano is often too prominent.

    2.   The first movement begins with a slow introduction which suggests the first theme of the following Allegro. The first theme is repeated twice. The second theme (G minor) is accented on the second beat with the imitation between the piano and strings. Material from the Introduction begins the Development (D minor) which uses the first and second themes. The Coda introduces a new theme (piu agitato).

    3.   The Scherzo in G minor is an extended movement based on one theme with two contrasting Trios.

    4.   The Andante cantabile in B-flat major reveals Schumann's melodic gifts. The melody begins after a three-measure introduction by the cello, which has the bass string tuned down from C to B-flat. The opening of the Finale is anticipated by characteristic falling fifths at the close of the movement.

    5.   The Finale in E-flat major begins with the interval of a fifth followed by a fugato section, announced by the viola. The cantabile second theme is introduced by the cello. A short subsidiary theme appears in imitation between the piano and viola, then cello and violin. The movement continues with the fugal theme in stretto; a new theme in A-flat major appears in the piano; a return of the fugato section.

C.   Three Trios for Piano, Violin, Cello (*M* 1, p. 287)

    1.   Op. 63 in D minor (1847); Op. 80 in F major (1847); Op. 110 in G minor (1851)

        a.   Characteristics include sudden changes of mood, full harmony in piano with strings doubling the outer parts, antiphonal effects, dotted note rhythms, compound rhythmic figures, changes in tempo, syncopation, energetic movements, vague and formless movements, uneven quality and use of the falling fifth motive (Op. 110).

D.   *Fantasiestücke*, Op. 88 (1842) (piano, violin, cello)

    1.   Romanza, Humoresque, Duet, March

        a.   One of the lesser works, with much use of doubling, sequence and a loose form.

E.   *Märchenerzählungen* (1853) (piano, clarinet, viola)

    1.   Four contrasting movements which lack vitality, but use interesting combinations of unusual color.

SELECTED BIBLIOGRAPHY

Books

1.   Abraham, Gerald, ed. *Schumann, A Symposium*. New York: Oxford University Press, 1952. (Chamber Music: pp. 138-175)

2.   Basch, Victor. *Schumann, A Life of Suffering*, tr. Catherine Alison Phillips. New York: Alfred A. Knopf, 1931.

3.   Bedford, Herbert. *Robert Schumann, His Life and Work*. New York: Harper, 1925.

4.   Boucoureschliev, André. *Schumann*, tr. Arthur Boyars. New York: Grove Press, 1959.

5.   Chissell, Joan Q. *Schumann*. London: J. M. Dent, 1967; New York: Farrar, Straus and Cudahy, 1967. (Chamber Music: pp. 166-179)

6.   Einstein, Alfred. *Music in the Romantic Era*. New York: W. W. Norton, 1947.

7.   Evans, Edwin. *Schumann*. London: Novello, 1944.

8. Fuller-Maitland, John Alexander. *Schumann: Concerted Chamber Music*. London: Oxford University Press, 1929.

9. –––––––*Schumann*. New York: Scribner, 1913. (reprint: Port Washington, NY: Kennikat Press, 1970)

10. Mason, Daniel Gregory. *The Romantic Composers*. New York: Macmillan, 1926.

11. Niecks, Frederick. *Robert Schumann*. New York: E. P. Dutton, 1925.

12. Peyser, Herbert F. *Robert Schumann, Tone-poet, Prophet, and Critic*. New York: Philharmonic Symphony Society, 1948.

13. Reissmann, August. *The Life and Works of Robert Schumann*, tr. Abby Langdon Alger. London: G. Bell, 1908.

14. Schauffler, Robert H. *Florestan: the Life and Work of Robert Schumann*. New York: Dover Publications, 1964. (Chamber Music: pp. 439-474)

15. *Thematisches Verzeichnis sämmtlicher im Druck erschienenen Werke Robert Schumanns*. London: H. Baron, 1966.

16. Schumann, Robert. *Music and Musician*, tr. Fanny Raymond Richter. London: W. Reeves, 1880.

17. Stork, Karl, ed. *The Letters of Robert Schumann*, tr. Hannah Bryant. New York: E. P. Dutton, 1907.

18. Walker, Alan, ed. *Robert Schumann the Man and His Music*. New York: Harper & Row, 1972. (Chamber Music: pp. 200-240)

19. Wasielewski, Joseph W. van. *Life of Robert Schumann*, tr. Abby Langdon Alger. Detroit: Information Coordinators, 1975. (reprint: 1871 edition)

20. Young, Percy M. *Tragic Muse: The Life and Works of Robert Schumann*. London: Dennis Dobson, 1961. (Chamber Music: pp. 136-147)

Articles

1. Beechey, Gwilym E. "Rhythmic Interpretation; Mozart, Beethoven, Schubert and Schumann." *MR* 33 (1972), pp. 233-248.

2. Davies, Fanny. "On Schumann–and Reading Between the Lines." *ML* 6 (1925), pp. 214-223.

3. Geirginer, Karl. "Farewell of a Genius." *Mus Am* 63 (Feb 10, 1943), pp. 24, 213.

4. Schumann, Eugene. "The Diary of Robert and Clara Schumann." *ML* 15 (1934), pp. 287-300.

5. Redlich, Hans F. "Schumann Discoveries; A Postscript [Piano Quintet in C minor]." *Monthly Musical Record* 80 (Dec 1950), pp. 261-265; 81 (Jan 1951), pp. 14-16.

Music

Study (Miniature) Scores

1. *Miscellaneous Chamber Works*, ed. Albert E. Wier. Melville, NY: Belwin-Mills, 1973.
2. String Quartet, Op. 41: *EE* 74, 75, 76; *KSS* 1105; *Ph* 361, 362, 363.
3. Piano Trios, Op. 63, 80: *KSS* 1107.
4. Piano Trios, Op. 88, 110, 132: *EE* 86, 87, 88; *KSS* 1108.
5. Piano Quartet, Op. 47: *EE* 77; *KSS* 1106.
6. Piano Quintet, Op. 44: *EE* 78; *KSS* 1106.

Playing Parts and Scores

7. String Quartets, Op. 41: *CE*, Series 4; *PE* 2379; New York: International Music Company, 1944.
8. Piano Trios, Op. 63, 80, 110: *CE*, Series 5, v. 2; *PE* 2377.
9. Piano Quartet, Op. 47: *CE*, Series 5, v. 1; *PE* 2380.
10. Piano Quintet, Op. 44: *CE*, Series 5, v. 1; *PE* 2381.
11. *Fantasiestücke*, Op. 88: *PE* 2378.
12. Sonata in A minor for Piano and Violin, Op. 105: *PE* 2367.
13. (*CE*) *Schumann sämtlicher Werke*, in 14 Series, ed. Clara Schumann. Leipzig: Breitkopf & Härtel, 1879-1893. (reprint: Farnborough, Hantshire, England: Gregg Press, 1968; New York: E. F. Kalmus, in 64 volumes)

OUTLINE VIII

JOHANNES BRAHMS (1833 - 1897)

I. **Life**

1833   Born in Hamburg, May 7. Studied music with his father, a double-bass player and Eduard Marxsen.
1847   Made his debut as a pianist playing his own music.
1853   Accompanist for the Hungarian violinist Eduard Reményi. Met Joseph Joachim and Robert Schumann.
1857   Pianist and conductor for the Prince of Lippe-Detmolds. Studied in Hamburg (1860-1862).
1862   Conductor of the *Singakademie* in Vienna (1862-1864).
1864   Lived in Hamburg, Zürich, Baden-Baden, Vienna. Made concert tours. Met with increasing artistic and financial success.
1871   Conductor of orchestral concerts of "Friends of Music" (1871-1874). Vienna became his permanent home (1878). Refused an honorary Doctor of Music degree from Cambridge University, but accepted a Doctor of Philosophy degree from the University of Breslau (1881).
1891   Visited Meiningen and heard the clarinetist, Richard Mühlfeld. He was so impressed with his playing that he decided to compose chamber music using the instrument.
1897   Died in Vienna, April 3.

II. **Catalogue of Chamber Music**

A. String Instruments
    1. Three Quartets for 2 violins, viola, cello
    2. Two Quintets for 2 violins, 2 violas, cello
    3. Two Sextets for 2 violins, 2 violas, 2 cellos
B. One Quintet for clarinet, 2 violins, viola, cello
C. Piano with Instruments
    1. Sonatas
        a. Three for piano, violin
        b. Two for piano, cello
        c. Two for piano, clarinet
    2. Trios
        a. Three for piano, violin, cello
        b. One for piano, clarinet, cello
        c. One for piano, horn, violin
    3. Three Quartets for piano, violin, viola, cello
    4. One Quintet for piano, 2 violins, viola, cello

III. **Chamber Music**

A. Brahms wrote twenty-four chamber music works. His first chamber work was a Trio, Op. 8, for piano, violin, cello (1854). He restored the clarity of classicism and completed the classical school of Haydn, Mozart and middle period Beethoven. His forms are classical with an occasional suggestion of romanticism. Twenty early quartets were destroyed before Op. 51 appeared (1873). Some early works were rewritten.
B. His themes are generally simple, but he invested them with great meaning. He used germ

motives; themes evolving around one note; themes on successive notes of a chord (sometimes omitting one note); themes borrowed from songs. Motives from the subject were often divided between answering instruments. Themes are idiomatic for the instruments.

C.   His harmony is based on the devices of the period: seventh chords, augmented sixths and triads predominate. Parallel thirds and sixths are a favorite device.

D.   Complex rhythms are characteristic (two against three and more involved combinations) and four-measure patterns are often avoided. Off-beat accents are frequent. His favorite rhythms are dactylic ($- \cup \cup$) and anapestic ($\cup \cup -$).

E.   He favored traditional sonata-form, often treated in a highly dramatic way. He was a master of variation and used the rondo form in a variety of patterns. His third movements may be quiet or loud, but they are rarely capricious.

F.   He frequently used many themes in polyphonic style, sometimes giving a thick texture to the music. Figurations in contrary motion and arpeggios are used in many ways. The cyclic idea is used.

G.   His music is usually divided into four periods. He often worked on a composition for years with many revisions and destroyed all unfinished and unpublished manuscripts.

   1.   Early Period (up to 1855)
      a.   Trio, Op. 8 (1854; revised 1891)
   2.   Transition Period (1855-1865)
      a.   String Sextet, Op. 18
      b.   Piano Quartets, Op. 25, Op. 26
      c.   Piano Quintet, Op. 34
      d.   String Sextet, Op. 36
      e.   Sonata for Piano, Cello, Op. 38
      f.   Trio for Piano, Violin, Horn, Op. 40
   3.   Mature Period (1865-1890)
      a.   Quartets, Op. 51, Nos. 1, 2
      b.   Piano Quartet, Op. 60
      c.   String Quartet, Op. 67
      d.   Sonata for Piano, Violin, Op. 78
      e.   Trio for Piano, Violin, Cello, Op. 87
      f.   String Quintet, Op. 88
      g.   Sonata for Piano, Cello, Op. 99
      h.   Sonata for Piano, Violin, Op. 100
      i.   Trio for Piano, Violin, Cello, Op. 101
      j.   Sonata for Piano, Violin, Op. 108
      k.   String Quintet, Op. 111
   4.   Late Period (1890-1895)
      a.   Trio for Piano, Clarinet, Cello, Op. 114
      b.   Sonata for Piano, Clarinet, Op. 120, Nos. 1 and 2

IV. String Quartets

A.   Op. 51, No. 1 in C minor (1873) (*M* 1, p. 127)
   1.   A sonorous, dramatic work written on broad symphonic lines. The cyclic idea is used in the Romanze and Finale. The first, second and fourth movements are based on two contrasting motives, rising and falling, which unite in a single idea.
   2.   Allegro (C minor). Sonata-form.
      a.   In 3/2 time. The first theme is in a dotted quarter- and eighth-note rhythm (meas. 1-10). The second theme is based on a falling motive (meas. 11-12). A third theme appears in measure 62 and a bridge section based on the first theme (meas. 83-86) leads to the Development (meas. 87-137). The Recapitulation (meas. 137) uses material similar to the Exposition and the movement closes with a Coda (meas. 227) based on the first theme.

3.   Romanze, poco Adagio (A-flat major)
    a.   Related to the first movement by a dotted eighth- and sixteenth-note rhythm. Effective use of the third relationship (C major) (meas. 13-14). The middle section is in A-flat minor, with the characteristic use of empty first beats (meas. 27). The first theme returns in the three lower instruments (meas. 49), followed by the middle section theme and a Coda using the first theme (meas. 86).
4.   Allegretto molto moderato e comodo (F minor)
    a.   The viola, one of Brahms' favorite instruments, is featured. Typical chromatic theme (meas. 15). In movement III the Trio (un poco animato) uses the "bariolage" effect in the second violin. Triplets in the passage marked "lusingando" (meas. 38) are combined later with the first theme (meas. 55).
5.   Allegro (C minor)
    a.   The first theme is related to the first theme of the first movement. The second theme (meas. 70) has the same three notes as the first theme, but is in E-flat major and in a quiet rhythm.
B.   Op. 51, No. 2 in A minor (1873) (*M* 1, p. 138)
    1.   Lyric style with contrasting passages. All movements are in A major or A minor. This is the only Minuet in Brahms' chamber works.
    2.   Allegro non troppo (A minor)
        a.   Begins with a motto theme said to be Joachim's: (A) - F - A - E ("*Frei aber einsam*" [Free but lonely]). The second theme (meas. 46), in thirds and sixths, is one of Brahms' most attractive. The Development is a compressed working over of measures 1-3. The Recapitulation enters on the weak beat (meas. 183), preceded by the inversion of the F - A - E theme in the viola. The Coda (meas. 287) introduces the motto theme in retrograde (meas. 323-328).
    3.   Andante moderato (A major)
        a.   In large A - B - A form. The A section is in three parts (a - meas. 1-8 – b - meas. 9-18 – a - meas. 18-30). The B section (meas. 43-76) is in two parts (meas. 43-60 – meas. 60-76); the second part is an elaboration of measures 1-8. The A section (meas. 77-110) is a Recapitulation. Coda (meas. 111-124).
    4.   Quasi Minuetto, moderato
        a.   In three parts. Much use of syncopation and cross accents. Part I is in three sections (meas. 1-16 – meas. 16-28 – meas. 28-40), all based on measures 1-16. Part II is a polyphonic Trio in 2/4 time interrupted by a transitory passage, with two themes in canon. A transitory passage, again in canon, leads to Part III, a da capo (meas. 134). Coda (meas. 168).
    5.   Allegro non assai
        a.   Rondo with elements of sonata-form. Second theme (meas. 44); closing section (meas. 59-75); suggestion of opening theme (meas. 75-100). Development with a suggestion of a Recapitulation (meas. 100-198); first theme (meas. 116); second theme (meas. 143). Recapitulation (meas. 198-293). The Coda (meas. 293-359) uses the first theme in canon and a theme suggesting Schumann's *Quartet in A minor* (meas. 320), concluding with the first theme in diminution (Più vivace).
C.   Op. 67 in B-flat major (1875) (*M* 1, p. 169)
    1.   A contrast to the first two quartets. Full of humor; use of cross accents, syncopation, rhythmic counterpoint, hemiola rhythm.
    2.   Vivace (B-flat major)
        a.   Sonata-form. The first theme, in 6/8 time, is like a horn call. Hemiola rhythm (meas. 10-12); a humorous stopping of the theme on the third eighth note begins the transition (meas. 21-31). The second theme group begins in measure 31. A third theme enters (meas. 58) in 2/4 time, which returns to 6/8 (meas. 60-63) and then to 2/4.
        b.   Development (meas. 103-204), in 6/8 and 2/4 times. The material is largely derived

from the first and second themes of the Exposition with change of signature from two flats to three sharps (meas. 127) and back again (meas. 161). There is a wide range of modulation.

    c.   Recapitulation (meas. 205) is similar to the Exposition. The Coda (meas. 310) is a highly developed section which combines most of the previous material. The combination of 6/8 and 2/4 time appears at the beginning of the Coda (meas. 312).

3.   Andante (F major)
    a.   Three-part form. The least successful movement of the quartet.

4.   Agitato (Allegretto non troppo) (D minor)
    a.   Scherzo movement. The viola is prominent and the other instruments use mutes. The Trio (meas. 130) is a neutral contrasting section. The final cadence is especially effective harmonically.

5.   Poco Allegretto con Variazioni (B-flat major)
    a.   One of Brahms' finest quartet movements. It consists of a folk-like theme with eight variations and Coda. All the instruments take part in playing the three-part theme in its various shapes. The key changes give additional color. The first theme of the first movement returns in measure 95. The second theme of the first movement appears in measure 132. From measure 150 to the end, the triplet first theme and the variation theme are combined in various ways.

V.   Two String Quartets

A.   Op. 88 in F major for 2 Violins, 2 Violas, Cello (1882) (*M* 1, p. 193)
    1.   Allegro non troppo ma con brio (F major)
        a.   The first theme group (meas. 1-21) has a short contrasting section in D major (meas. 9). The second theme, in triple rhythm, enters in the viola in A major (meas. 9). It appears in the first violin (meas. 57) with the same two-against-three rhythm. The Development (meas. 111-137) has an unusually long anticipation (meas. 77-110). Key contrasts of F major and A major are also used in the Finale.

    2.   Grave ed appassionato (C-sharp minor) - Allegretto vivace (A major)
        a.   This movement is a combination of a slow movement and a Scherzo with alternating Grave (C-sharp minor) and Allegretto vivace (A major) sections. A remarkable passage begins with the theme in the cello (meas. 176), and the movement concludes unexpectedly in A major.

    3.   Allegro energico (F major)
        a.   Sonata-form with fugal sections. The brief fugue is followed by an augmentation of the first measure of the theme (meas. 23-26). The first three notes of the fugue theme become increasingly important. The second theme in A major (meas. 34) acts as a countersubject to the fugue theme. The Development (meas. 55) introduces (meas. 63) a chromatic theme, in triple rhythm and minor mode, which is derived from the fugue subject. The Coda (meas. 146) uses material from the fugue subject, beginning with an expansion of the first three notes.

B.   Op. 111 in G major for 2 Violins, 2 Violas, Cello (1890) (*M* 1, p. 216)
    1.   Allegro non troppo, ma con brio (G major)
        a.   An outstanding movement. The opening theme is in the cello. The bridge passage (meas. 21) gives prominence to the interval of a third. The second theme is in two parts (first part, meas. 26; second part, meas. 38). There is a complex Development in five contrasting sections. Recapitulation (meas. 106). The Coda uses the first part of the main theme in the cello with the rising third motive (meas. 162).

    2.   Adagio (D minor)
        a.   The lyric main theme is treated without contrasting sections. It is developed in G major, reaches a climax in D major and returns to D minor at the Coda (meas. 69).

    3.   Un poco Allegretto (G minor)

    a.   The first section is a twelve-measure melody repeated. This melody is based on a falling second; sequential patterns. The section section (meas. 25) introduces a new motive, a rising third, which is imitated by the viola. Modulations lead through B-flat major to G minor (meas. 44). The Trio (meas. 61) in G major has a folk-like theme which is given to violas and violins alternately.

4.   Vivace ma non troppo presto (G major)

    a.   A Hungarian peasant-dance Finale. The main theme is introduced in measure 13; the second theme in measure 51. These tunes are used in many ways. The main theme appears in the final animato (meas. 248).

VI.   Two String Sextets

A.   Op. 18 in B-flat major for 2 Violins, 2 Violas, 2 Cellos (1860)   (*M* 1, p. 22)

    1.   The first of Brahms' published chamber works; some revisions were suggested by Joachim.

    2.   Allegro ma non troppo (B-flat major)

      a.   Three principal themes: 1) measure 1; 2) measure 61; 3) measure 107. The themes all have their own special rhythmic character. The second theme (meas. 61), in A major, is in the style of a Viennese waltz.

      b.   The themes are often suggested before they appear; modifications of the themes when repeated are a characteristic treatment (change from F-sharp minor to F minor, meas. 76, 78).

    3.   Andante, ma moderato (D minor)

      a.   Theme and variations. This form is used six times in the chamber works.

    4.   Scherzo (F major)

      a.   An unusually short, energetic movement in Beethoven style. Use of modifications of the theme (B-flat minor, meas. 45; B minor, meas. 49).

    5.   Poco Allegretto e grazioso (B-flat major)

      a.   Rondo form. The main theme is in the style of Haydn, with the cello featured. It shows Brahms' skill in developing each phrase from the preceding one.

B.   Op. 36 in G major for 2 Violins, 2 Violas, 2 Cellos (1864) (*M* 1, p. 97)

    1.   Allegro non troppo

      a.   This sextet is lighter in texture, more profound, polyphonic and less complex than some of the preceding works and represents a new style development.

      b.   Rising fifths at the beginning of the first theme are the basis of the whole movement. The viola repeats the notes G, F-sharp through the first thirty-two measures in spite of harmonic clashes. The Development (meas. 217) uses a motive of fifths in all instruments; brilliant contrapuntal treatment; opens in D minor, modulates to the remote key of C-sharp minor.

    2.   Scherzo (G minor)

      a.   Three sections: Scherzo (meas. 1-120); Trio (meas. 121-250); Scherzo (meas. 251-371). The Scherzo is also in three parts: Part I (meas. 1-33); Part II (meas. 34-68); Part III (meas. 69-120).

      b.   The material for the movement is derived from two motives (meas. 1-4; meas. 17-20). In measure 21 the cello plays the second motive accompanied by the first motive in inversion and with shifted rhythm. In measure 25 the two motives are combined again. Part II (meas. 34-56) has a motive generated from measure 31; it uses a rest for the first beat. At measure 51, two motives are combined and developed in imitation. In measure 58, the return of the first motive is prepared in a major tonality. The Trio (meas. 121) theme is a peasant dance; a contrasting theme (meas. 164) is derived from the Trio theme.

    3.   Poco Adagio (E minor)

      a.   This theme and variations is one of Brahms' greatest movements. The theme is in

three parts: 1) measure 1-5; 2) measures 6-8; 3) measure 9-12. The variations are complex and frequently based on the harmony rather than the melody.
  4. Poco Allegro (G major)
  a. Effective beginning out of the key, leading to a broad cantabile melody (meas. 7).

VII. Two Quintets

A. Op. 115 in B minor for Clarinet in A, 2 Violins, Viola, Cello (1891) (*M* 1, p. 240)
  1. This quintet is a great work, revealing Brahms' simplicity of material and his power to develop and give this material a meaning which is universal in its scope.
  2. Allegro (B minor)
  a. First theme group (meas. 1-24). The second theme (meas. 37) is built on three notes of the scale: G, F-sharp, E. The Development (meas. 71-135) uses the first motive; at the Quasi sostenuto (meas. 98) a bridge theme enters in D-flat major; a rhythmic figure (meas. 99) is developed; modulations through B-flat major, D-flat major, A major, F major, C major to F-sharp major (meas. 121). From measure 123, the rhythmic figure is answered in inversion. Recapitulation (meas. 136). The Coda (meas. 195) begins with the first theme and the second theme motive is heard. The last twelve measures are one of Brahms' finest inspirations.
  3. Adagio (B major)
  a. Three-part form. Part II (meas. 52) is evolved from the first three notes of the first part. Rhapsodic, Hungarian-like treatment of the material. Part III (meas. 88) is almost like Part I. The Coda (meas. 128) begins with a phrase on the clarinet, which is also derived from the first three notes of Part I.
  4. Andantino (D major)
  a. Strong contrast between the lyric Andantino (D major) section and the Presto non assai (B minor). The staccato motive of the Presto is derived from the first four notes of the Andantino.
  5. Finale, con moto (B minor)
  a. Theme and five variations. The theme of the first movement returns in measure 193.
B. Op. 34 in B minor for Piano, 2 Violins, Viola, Cello (1864) (*M* 1, p. 78)
  1. Originally written as a quintet with two cellos; rewritten for two pianos and finally as a piano quintet.
  2. Allegro non troppo (F minor)
  a. Powerful first theme; bridge theme (meas. 23); second theme in the piano (meas. 34); concluding theme (meas. 74). The themes are usually prepared in the cadence of the preceding theme. Masterful treatment of a variety of rhythms.
  b. Recapitulation (meas. 166) is prepared in measure 160. A three-note motive without the first beat (meas. 248); the first theme is varied and treated in imitation (meas. 261); first theme in the cello (meas. 271). Coda (meas. 283).
  3. Andante, un poco Adagio (A-flat major)
  a. A - B - A form. A lyric movement, with a rhythmic melody in thirds and sixths; alternating between major and minor; rhythmic interest lies in the left-hand part and strings; the first theme is suggested after the middle section (meas. 55); return in measure 75.
  4. Scherzo (C minor)
  1. Strong rhythmic drive. The use of duple meter is unusual in the chamber music Scherzos of Brahms. An example of unity with variety. Four themes, rhythmically contrasted, are used: 1) measure 2; 2) measure 13; 3) measure 23; 4) Trio, measure 194.
  5. Finale (F minor)
  a. Sonata-form without a formal Development. The first theme (meas. 42) follows the

introduction and goes through many transformations in the course of the movement. Second theme (meas. 95). The concluding section is in syncopated triplets (meas. 138). A new version of the first theme (meas. 62) appears in C minor. Another variant (meas. 322) leads to the last transformation of the theme in the Coda (meas. 343). The second and first themes appear separately and in combination.

SELECTED BIBLIOGRAPHY

Books

1. Brahms, Johannes. *The Herzogenberg Correspondence*, ed. Max Kalbeck, tr. Hannah Bryant. New York: Vienna House, 1971.
2. Brahms, Johannes, and Theodor Billroth. *Letters from a Musical Friendship*, tr. Hans Barkan. Norman: University of Oklahoma Press, 1957.
3. Drinker, Henry S. *The Chamber Music of Brahms*. Philadelphia: Elkan-Vogel, 1932.
4. Geiringer, Karl. *Brahms. His Life and Work*. New York: Houghton Mifflin, 1936; London: Allen & Unwin, 1948.
5. Fuller-Maitland, John Alexander. *Johannes Brahms*. London: Methuen, 1911. (Chamber Music: pp. 105-130)
6. Jacobson, Bernard. *The Music of Johannes Brahms*. Cranbury, NJ: Farleigh Dickinson University Press, 1977.
7. Latham, Peter. *Brahms*, 3rd edition. London: J. M. Dent, 1975. (Chamber Music: pp. 120-132)
8. Mason, Daniel Gregory. *The Chamber Music of Brahms*. New York: Macmillan, 1933. (reprint: Ann Arbor: J. W. Edwards, 1950)
9. Niemann, Walter. *Brahms, A Comprehensive View of the Man and an Exhaustive Critique of His Works*, tr. Catherine Alison Philips. New York: Alfred A. Knopf, 1929; New York: Tudor Publishing Co., 1937. (Chamber Music: pp. 256-301)

Articles

1. Abert, Hermann. "Bach, Beethoven, Brahms," tr. Frederick H. Martens. *MQ* 13 (1927), pp. 329-343.
2. Dunhill, Thomas F. "Brahms Quintet for Piano and Strings, Op. 23." *MT* 72 (1931), p. 319.
3. Pulver, Jeffrey. "Chamber Music by Brahms in the Breitkopf edition." *Strad* 44 (1933), pp. 144, 146.
4. ——————"The String Music of Johannes Brahms." *Strad* 43 (1933), pp. 28, 59, 99.
5. Redlich, Hans F. "Bruckner and Brahms Quartets in F." *ML* 36 (1955), pp. 253-258.
6. Tovey, Donald F. "Brahms Chamber Music" in *Essays and Lectures on Music*, pp. 220-270. London: Oxford University Press, 1949.
7. Truscott, Harold. "Brahms and Sonata Style [Sextet for Strings, Op. 18]," *MR* 25 (1964), pp. 186-201.

Music

Study (Miniature) Score

1. *The Chamber Music of Brahms*, ed. Albert E. Wier. Melville, NY: Belwin-Mills, 1973.
2. String Quartets, Op. 51, Nos. 1 & 2, Op. 67: *EE Chamber Music Complete*, v. 1; *KSS* 799; *Lea* 168; *Ph* 372, 373, 374.
3. String Quartet in A minor, Op. 51, No. 2: *BH* 220.
4. String Quintets, Op. 88, 111: *EE Chamber Music Complete*, v. 1; *KSS* 799; *Lea* 169.
5. String Sextets, Op. 18, 36: *EE Chamber Music Complete*, v. 1; *KSS* 1148; *Lea* 170.
6. Piano Trios: *EE Chamber Music Complete*, v. 2; Op 8: *KSS* 776; Op. 87, 101: *KSS* 1239; Op. 40, 114: *KSS* 1240.
7. Piano Quartets, Op. 25, 26: *EE Chamber Music Complete*, v. 2; *KSS* 773, 775.
8. Piano Quintet, Op. 34: *EE Chamber Music Complete*, v. 2; *KSS* 800.
9. Clarinet Quintet, Op. 115: *BH* 208; *EE Chamber Music Complete*, v. 1; *KSS* 727; *Lea* 169.

Playing Parts and Scores

10. String Quartets, Op. 51, Nos. 1 & 2, Op 67: *CE*, v. 7; *Edwin F. Kalmus Chamber Music Series*, No. 4; *IMC*; *PE* 3903.
11. String Quintets, Op. 88, 111: *CE*, v. 7; *IMC*; *PE* 3905a/b.
12. String Sextets, Op. 18, 36: *CE* v. 7; *IMC*; *PE* 3906a/b.
13. Piano Trios, Op. 8, 40, 87, 101, 114: *CE*, v. 9; *PE* 3898 (all together); *PE* 3899a-e (separately).
14. Piano Trio, Op. 8. Wiesbaden: Breitkopf & Härtel, No. 6051.
15. Piano Trios, Op. 40, 87, 114. New York: International Music Company, 1946.
16. Piano Quartets, Op. 25, 26, 60: *CE*, v. 8; *PE* 3904 (all together); *PE* 3939a/b/c (separately).
17. Piano Quintet. Op. 34: *CE*, v. 8; *PE* 3660; Munich: G. Henle Verlag, 1971.
18. Clarinet Quintet, Op. 115: *CE*, v. 7; *PE* 3905c.
19. Sonatas for Violin and Piano, Op. 78, 100, 108. Wiesbaden: Breitkopf & Härtel, Nos. 6036, 6037, 6038; Munich: G. Henle Verlag; New York: G. Schirmer, 1918.
20. Sonatas for Cello and Piano, Op. 38, 99. Munich: G. Henle Verlag; New York: International Music Company, 1948.
21. Sonatas for Clarinet (or Viola) and Piano, Op. 120, Nos. 1 & 2. New York: International Music Company, 1948; *PE* 3896a.
22. (*CE*) *Johannes Brahms sämtliche Werke*, in 26 volumes, ed. Hans Gál and Eusibius Mandyczewski. Wiesbaden: Breitkopf & Härtel, 1927. (reprint: New York: E. F. Kalmus, in 55 volumes)
23. *Complete Chamber Music for Strings and Clarinet Quintet*. New York: Dover Publications. (reprint: Breitkopf & Härtel)

OUTLINE IX

BEDŘICH [FRIEDRICH] SMETANA (1824 - 1884)

I. Life

1824   Born in Leitomischl, Bohemia, March 2. Due to his father's opposition, Smetana was largely self-taught in music.

1843   Went to Prague. Studied theory and piano with Josef Proksch and gave music lessons.

1846   Took part in the Revolution of 1848 when Austria granted Bohemia political independence. Became strongly nationalistic. Received permission to establish a school of music, which he did with the financial help of Franz Liszt.

1849   Married Katharina Kolař, an accomplished pianist. She died in Dresden in 1859 on a trip from Sweden.

1856   Went to Götheborg, Sweden, as conductor of the Philharmonic Society. Composed symphonic tone poems.

1861   Returned to Prague and became active in the establishment of a national opera house. Composed a number of successful operas (*The Bartered Bride*, 1866).

1874   Resigned as conductor of the Prague opera because of political opposition and the strong criticism of his operas after 1868. He developed a nervous disorder and became totally deaf (1874). Turned to composition of symphonic poems (*My Country*, 1874-1879) and wrote his famous string quartet in E minor, *Aus meinem Leben* (From My Life).

1884   Died insane in Prague, May 12.

II. Chamber Music

A.   Smetana composed only three chamber works: Piano Trio, Op. 15 in G minor (1855); String Quartet in E minor ("From My Life") (1876); Second String Quartet in D minor (1882).

B.   He is often referred to as the father of Bohemian music and was a leader in the development of a national school of composition. His music is descriptive, programmatic and always dramatic.

C.   String Quartet in E minor ("From My Life") (1876) (*M* 1, p. 182)

    1.   Smetana, himself, explained the program of this quartet.

      a.   Movement I: his youth in the country, a fate motive.

      b.   Movement II: a merry life in the village and castle.

      c.   Movement III: a love scene, thoughts of his first wife.

      d.   Movement IV: his joy in work is interrupted by the tragedy of deafness, resignation.

    2.   Smetana said that the "four instruments should converse together in an intimate circle about the things which so deeply trouble me."

    3.   Allegro vivo appassionato (E minor)

      a.   Depicts his youth, love of art, romantic yearnings and a fateful warning of his future.

      b.   Modified sonata-form. The agitated first subject (fate motive) is stated in the viola (meas. 4). The romantic second subject (meas. 71) is in G major. The first four quarter notes of this subject furnish material for the following passages.

      c.   The Development begins (meas. 122) with the first subject in the first violin, answered by the cello (meas. 128). After a frenzied climax the music subsides (meas. 165) and the first part of the second subject is heard in the cello.

    d.   The Recapitulation (meas. 180) in E major uses only the second theme. Fragments of the first and second themes appear in the Coda (meas. 226).

4.   Allegro moderato a la Polka (F major)

    a.   Smetana wrote, "This movement recalls memories of my merry life in my youth when I used to write dance music and was known myself as an enthusiastic dancer."

    b.   Rondo form: A - B - A - B - A - Coda. The A sections are in F major and the B sections in D-flat major. In the first A section a second theme is introduced in the viola (meas. 39) and the first theme returns (meas. 67). The first B section (meas. 85) features a striking change in rhythm which Smetana said represented the aristocratic circles in which he lived.

5.   Largo sostenuto (A-flat major)

    a.   Memories of his first love who afterward became his wife.

    b.   Form A - B - A - B. There are two principal themes in this movement. The first A theme (meas. 7), in the first violin, is preceded by an expressive solo for cello (meas. 1). The B theme appears in the first violin (meas. 46). After a cadenza for the first violin (meas. 58) the first part of the A theme is heard fortissimo, leading into the second A section with the theme in the cello (meas. 68). The B section is heard again in A-flat major (meas. 76) and the movement closes with a restatement of the A theme in the viola (meas. 84).

6.   Vivace (E major)

    a.   "Joy over the discovery of how to treat national material in music. Then the beginning of deafness and a glimpse into the melancholy future."

    b.   The first group has two principal ideas, both strongly rhythmic (meas. 1; meas. 10). The second theme, scherzoso, (meas. 37) is used in various ways and leads to a return of the second idea fortissimo (meas. 77). The scherzoso theme is used again (meas. 101).

    c.   The Recapitulation (meas. 139) presents the material of the Exposition with the scherzoso theme in the tonic (E major). At the Più mosso (meas. 195) the first idea is given to the violins in tenths, followed by an energetic statement of the scherzoso theme over a tonic pedal.

    d.   After a two-measure rest, the mood changes abruptly in measure 222. An e'''', sustained by the first violin over tremolo strings, represents the approach of Smetana's deafness. "There is a ray of hope, but with a sense of sadness." The second theme of the first movement is heard (meas. 258). This theme alternates with the triplet figure of the first idea, pianissimo, as the quartet closes quietly.

SELECTED BIBLIOGRAPHY

Books

1.   Bartoš, František. *Bedřich Smetana: Letters and Reminiscences*, tr. Daphne Rusbridge. Prague: Artia, 1955.
2.   Clapham, John. *Smetana*. London: J. M. Dent, 1972. (Chamber Music: pp. 65-70)
3.   Karásek, Bohumil. *Bedřich Smetana*, tr. Joy Kadečková. Prague: Suprahon, 1967.
4.   Large, Brian. *Smetana*. London: Duckworth, 1970; New York: Praeger, 1970.
5.   Suermondt, R. P. *Smetana and Dvořák*. Stockholm: The Continental Book Co., 1949.

Article

1.   Weaver, William. "The Unknown Smetana." *HiFi/MA* 15 (May 1965), pp. 44-47.

Music

Study (Miniature) Scores

1. *Miscellaneous Chamber Works*, ed. Albert E. Wier. New York: Belwin-Mills, 1973.
2. String Quartet, No. 1: *EE* 275.
3. String Quartet, No. 2: *EE* 285.
4. Piano Trio, Op. 15: *EE* 335.

Playing Parts and Scores

5. String Quartet, No. 1: *PE* 2635; *IMC*.
6. Piano Trio, Op. 15: *PE* 4238.

OUTLINE X

ANTONÍN DVOŘÁK (1841 - 1904)

I. Life

1841   Born September 8 in Nehalozeves (Mühlhausen), Bohemia.

1857   Left home and entered the Prague Organ School where he studied with Karl F. Pitzsch. He graduated in 1862 and joined the National Theatre orchestra as a violist.

1873   First important composition, *Hymnus*, was performed on March 9 and attracted considerable attention.

1875   Awarded the Austrian State Prize for his *Symphony in E-flat* and began intensive work in composition. Friendship with Johannes Brahms, Franz Liszt and Hans von Bülow helped secure performances.

1884   Visited England several times and conducted his own works. Awarded an honorary Doctor of Music degree from Cambridge University (1891), and an honorary Doctor of Philosophy degree from Czech University in Prague (1890).

1891   Appointed professor of composition, instrumentation and music form at the Prague Conservatory.

1892   Became artistic director of the National Conservatory in New York (1892-1895). Visited a Bohemian community in Spillville, Iowa.

1893   Wrote his most famous work, a symphony *From the New World*.

1895   Returned to Prague as professor of composition at the Conservatory and became artistic director in 1901. Was the first musician to be made a life member of the Austrian House of Lords.

1904   Died in Prague, May 1.

II. Catalogue of Chamber Music

A. String Instruments
1. Eight string quartets (1874-1895)
2. Two string quintets, Op. 77 (1875), Op. 97 (1903)
3. One string sextet, Op. 48 (1878)

B. Piano and Strings
1. Four piano trios (1875-1891)
2. Two piano quartets, Op. 23 (1875), Op. 87 (1889)
3. One piano quintet, Op. 81 (1887)
4. Two sonatas for violin, piano, Op. 57 (1880), Op. 100 (1893)

C. Dvořák composed a total of about thirty chamber works, including those in manuscript.

III. Style

A. 1864-1874
1. There is a strong influence of Beethoven and Schubert up to 1870. From 1870 to 1874 the influence of Liszt and Wagner predominates.
2. Chamber works include five string quartets, one piano quintet, one string quintet.

B. 1874-1878
1. Dvořák returned to the classic composers as his models.
2. Chamber works include the string quartets Op. 16 in A minor, Op. 80 in E major, Op. 34 in D minor; string quintet Op. 77 in G major for 2 violins, viola, cello, bass; piano quartet Op. 23 in D major; piano trios Op. 21 in B-flat major, Op. 26 in G minor.

C. 1878-1890
1. This period marks the beginning of strong Slavic elements in his music.
2. A large number of chamber works were written, including a string sextet Op. 48 in A major; string quartets Op. 51 in E-flat major, Op. 61 in C major; piano trios Op. 65 in F minor, Op. 90 in E minor; piano quintet Op. 81 in A major; piano quartet Op. 87 in E-flat major.
D. 1892-1895
1. During this period Dvořák was in New York as artistic director of the National Conservatory.
2. The string quartet Op. 96 in F major, known as the "American Quartet" and the string quintet Op. 97 in E-flat major for two violins, two violas and cello were composed during his stay in the United States.
E. 1895-1904
1. He returned to Bohemia and wrote the quartets Op. 105 in A-flat major and Op. 106 in G major.
F. Dvořák was a versatile and prolific composer with a gift for spontaneous melodic invention and a sense of form. He made use of national folk tunes and rhythms and his works are frequently marked by strong emotional contrasts.

IV. **String Quartet, Op. 96 in F major, "American Quartet"** (*M* 1, p. 68)

A. Written while Dvořák was visiting the Bohemian community in Spillville, Iowa.
1. The work represents his impressions of folk music in America, but no authentic tunes are used.
B. Allegro ma non troppo (F major)
1. Sonata-form. A two-measure introduction is followed by the first theme which appears in the viola and then the violin. A subsidiary theme (meas. 26) leads to the second theme (meas. 44) in A major.
    a. The Development uses the themes of the Exposition. The Recapitulation (meas. 112) has the second theme in the tonic (meas. 156). An unusually short Coda concludes the movement.
C. Scherzo (F major)
1. This short movement is preceded by an expressive Lento (D minor).
2. The Scherzo is based on two sections which appear five times in alternation: I in F major (meas. 1-48); II in F minor (meas. 49-96); I in F major (meas. 97-148); II in F minor (meas. 149-191); I in F major (meas. 1-48). The second section uses the theme of the first section in augmentation.
D. The Finale, Vivace ma non troppo, is in rondo form with strongly contrasting sections.

V. **Piano Quintet, Op. 81 in A major (1887)** (*M* 1, p. 45)

A. The texture is generally harmonic and, possibly because Dvořák was a violist, the piano often plays a secondary role. The quintet is brilliant and colorful and his spontaneous melodic gifts are everywhere apparent.
B. Allegro ma non tanto
1. Sonata form. The quiet, expressive opening theme, alternating between the tonic major and minor (meas. 17), is given to the cello. A series of rapid modulations (C major - E minor - B major - E minor) in measures 29-39 is followed by two statements, the first varied, of the first subject (meas. 52; meas. 61). A transition (meas. 75) brings a sudden change of rhythm with a triplet figure and leads to the second theme (meas. 92) in C-sharp minor. This melody is the basis of the remainder of the Exposition.
2. The transition beginning in measure 138 leads to the Development (meas. 153) which opens with a figure in the bass. This is followed by a treatment of the beginning of the

first subject (meas. 167) and the following passage, and the second subject (meas. 208). A striking passage (meas. 255) introduces the Recapitulation (meas. 294).

   3.   In the Recapitulation the second subject (meas. 327) enters in F-sharp minor instead of the tonic key (A major). The movement closes with an exuberant Coda.

C.   *Dumka* (F-sharp minor)

   1.   The *dumka* (plural is *dumky*), a Russian word meaning "thought," is a type of Slavic folksong of elegiac character with strongly contrasting sections.

   2.   This *dumka* is in a rondo form: A - B - A - C - A - B transposed - A. The contrasting sections are separated by double bars. Considerable rhythmic complexity appears in the pochettino più mosso section (meas. 29) and the opening phrase appears transformed in the vivace section (meas. 108).

D.   Scherzo (Furiant) (A major)

   1.   A short sparkling movement with effective use of the high register of the piano (meas. 54-57), three against five in the piano (meas. 80-94) and colorful modulation (meas. 170-181).

E.   Finale: Allegro (A major)

   1.   Sonata-form without repetition of the Exposition. The principal theme of the first subject (meas. 12) is introduced by a theme which becomes an important part of the movement. The second subject, consisting of four themes, enters in the dominant (meas. 83). The first subject reappears (meas. 54) just before the Development.

   2.   The Development (meas. 163) is founded principally on the first subject. A brief fugato appears (meas. 224).

   3.   The Recapitulation (meas. 266) begins with the principal theme of the first subject. The second theme is in the usual tonic key (meas. 299) and a vigorous Coda concludes the movement.

SELECTED BIBLIOGRAPHY

Books

1.   Burghauser, Jarmil. *Antonín Dvořák*, tr. Jean Layton-Eislerová. Prague: Knihtisk, 1967.

2.   ——————*Antonín Dvořák; Thematic Catalogue, Bibliography, Survey of Life and Work.* London: Boosey & Hawkes, 1960.

3.   ——————*Antonín Dvořák Thematisches Verzeichnis.* Kassel: Alkor-Edition, 1960.

4.   Clapham, John. *Antonín Dvořák, Musician and Craftsman.* New York: St. Martin's Press, 1966. (Chamber Music: pp. 157-210)

5.   Fischl, Viktor. *Antonín Dvořák, His Achievement.* London: Linsay Drummon, 1943. (reprint: Westport, CT: Greenwood Press, 1970) (Chamber Music: pp. 111-126)

6.   Hadow, William Henry. *Studies in Modern Music.* London: Seeley & Co., 1904-1905.

7.   Hoffmeister, Karel. *Antonín Dvořák*, tr. Rosa Newmarch. London: John Lane, 1928.

8.   Hughes, Gervase. *Dvořák; His Life and Music.* New York: Dodd, Mead & Co., 1967.

9.   Robertson, Alec. *Dvořák.* New York: E. P. Dutton and Co., 1947. (Chamber Music: pp. 172-192)

10.   Šourek, Otakar. *Antonín Dvořák Letters and Reminiscences*, tr. Roberta Finlayson Samsour. Prague: Artia, 1954.

11.   Van Straaten, Jan [pseudonym of Barthold Fles]. *Slavonic Rhapsody: the Life of Antonín Dvořák.* New York: Allen, Towne and Heath, 1948.

Articles

1.   Beveridge, David. "Sophisticated primitivism: the significance of pentatonicism in Dvořák's 'American quartet'." *Current Mus* 24 (1977), pp. 25-36.

2. Colles, Henry C. "Antonín Dvořák." *MT* 82 (1941), pp. 130, 173, 209.
3. Hadow, William Henry. "Dvořák's Quintet for Pianoforte and Strings." *MT* 73 (1932), p. 401.
4. Hely-Hutchinson, Victor. "Dvořák the Craftsman." *ML* 22 (1941), pp. 303-312.
5. Hollander, H. "Dvořák the Czech." *ML* 22 (1941), pp. 313-317.
6. Lockspeiser, Edward. "The Dvořák Centenary." *ML* 22 (1941), pp. 299-302.
7. Nettl, Paul. "When Dvořák Came to the New World." *MC* 51 (Sept 1941), p. 5.
8. Newmarch, Rosa. "Anton Dvořák; a Plea for Remembrance." *Chesterian* 5 (1923), p. 97.
9. ––––––"The Letters of Dvořák to Hans Richter." *MT* 73 (1932), p. 605.

Music

Study (Miniature) Scores

1. *Miscellaneous Chamber Works*, ed. Albert E. Wier. Melville, NY: Belwin-Mills, 1973.
2. String Quartet in F major (American). New York: International Music Company.
3. String Quintet in G major, Op. 77: *EE* 338.
4. String Quintet in E-flat major, Op. 97: *EE* 306.
5. Piano Trio in F minor, Op. 65: *EE* 331.
6. Piano Trio in E minor (Dumky): *EE* 332.
7. Piano Quartet in E-flat major, Op. 87: *EE* 330.
8. Piano Quintet in A major, Op. 81: *EE* 305; Berlin: Simrock, 1888.

Playing Parts and Scores

9. String Quartet in D minor, Op. 34: *CE*, Series 4, v. 6; *PE* S-7314; *PE* D-819.
10. String Quartet in E-flat major, Op. 51. *CE*, Series 4, v. 6; New York: International Music Company, 1950; Prague: Supraphon, 1968.
11. String Quartet in C major, Op. 61. *CE*, Series 4, v. 7; New York: International Music Company, 1949.
12. String Quartet in F major, Op. 96. *CE*, Series 4, v. 7; New York: International Music Company, 1950.
13. String Quartet in A-flat major, Op. 105. *CE*, Series 4, v. 7; New York: International Music Company, 1948.
14. String Quartet in G major, Op. 106. *CE*, Series 4, v. 7; New York: International Music Company, 1952.
15. String Quintet in G major, Op. 77. *CE*, Series 4, v. 8; New York: International Music Company, n. d.
16. String Quintet in E-flat major, Op. 97. *CE*, Series 4, v. 8; New York: International Music Company, 1943.
17. String Sextet in A major, Op. 48. *CE*, Series 4, v. 8; New York: International Music Company, n. d.
18. Piano Trio in B-flat, Op. 21. *CE*, Series 4, v. 9; *PE* S-7327; *PE* D-808.
19. Piano Trio in G minor, Op. 26. *CE*, Series 4, v. 9; New York: International Music Company, 1955.
20. String Trio in F minor, Op. 65. *CE*, Series 4, v. 9; New York: International Music Company, 1952.
21. Piano Trio, Op. 90 (Dumky). *CE* Series 4, v. 9; New York: International Music Company, 1959; Prague, Supraphon, 1968.
22. Piano Quartet in D major, Op. 23. *CE*, Series 4, v. 10; *PE* S-7373; *PE* D-809.
23. Piano Quartet in E-flat major, Op. 87. *CE*, Series 4, v. 10; New York: International Music Company, 1947.
24. (*CE*) *Souborne vydani del Antonína Dvořáka* (Complete Works of Antonín Dvořák), 68 volumes, ed. Okatar Šourek. Prague: Artia, 1956.

OUTLINE XI

CÉSAR (-AUGUSTE) FRANCK (1822 - 1890)

I. Life

1822 Born at Liège in the Walloon region of Belgium, December 10. He became an accomplished pianist at an early age.

1833 Made his first concert tour of Belgium. Became a pupil of Antonín Reicha (harmony and counterpoint) in Paris (1835).

1837 Student at the Paris Conservatory with Aimé Leborne (counterpoint), Pierre Zimmermann (piano), and François Benoist (organ). Received the *Grand Prix d'Honneur* for piano (the first and only prize of the kind ever given); first prize for fugue (1840); second prize for organ (1841).

1842 Returned to Liège to begin his career as a composer; his father had wanted him to become a piano virtuoso. After two years in Belgium, he settled in Paris as a teacher (1844).

1851 Appointed organist of the church of Saint-Jean-Saint-François.

1853 Choirmaster at Sainte-Clotilde.

1858 Appointed organist at Sainte-Clotilde, a position which he held until his death. Experienced the Siege of Paris (1870).

1872 Succeeded his teacher (Benoist) as professor of organ at the Paris Conservatory. Named a *Chevalier de la Légion d'honneur* (1885).

1887 His works were presented at the "Franck Festival," sponsored by pupils and friends (January 30). The program, directed by Jules Pasdeloup, was well planned but poorly executed.

1890 He took part in the triumphal concert at Tournai with Eugène Ysaÿe. He was injured by a Paris omnibus while crossing a street, suffering complications which finally caused his death on November 8, 1890. Official coolness (marked during his life) continued after his death; neither the Ministry of Fine Arts nor the Conservatoire sent a representative to the funeral.

II. Musician and Composer

A. A simple, modest, good and warm-hearted man with a great capacity for work. He disregarded worldly considerations, displaying in his art the same strong faith as in his religion. His life was devoted entirely to teaching, composition and playing the organ.

B. He wrote a comparatively small number of important works and there is a wide difference in the quality of his music. Probably no composer of his rank was ever given so little recognition. His life was a consistent record of neglect, coupled with badly organized and technically inadequate performances.

C. As a composer he was characterized neither by nationalism nor program music. After 1862, he stopped marking opus numbers; Op. 22 is the last one employed.

D. The influence of his predecessors (Pierre Monsigny, Nicolas Dalayrac, André Ernest Grétry, Étienne Méhul) is shown in his early works, especially in types of melody and their treatments. At the same time, however, he used contemporary techniques and was affected by developments of his time.

E. Nineteenth-century French music was dominated by opera. Serious musicians, dissatisfied, followed the path marked out by Franck. Among his pupils were Vincent d'Indy, Ernest Chausson, Alexis de Castillon, Pierre de Bréville, Charles Bordes, Guillaume Lekeu, Henri Duparc, Gabriel Pierné, Joseph Guy-Ropartz, Augusta Holmès, Paul Vidal and

Charles Tournemire, all of whom helped toward the establishment of a school of modern French instrumental music. Franck exerted a great influence at the Conservatory. His organ classes were also a training school for composers, who were grounded upon Bach and Beethoven.

F. His creative life has been divided by d'Indy into three periods: 1) early works, trios, etc. (1841-1852), 2) works largely of religious character (1858-1874), 3) period of maturity and full possession of his artistic personality (1876-1890).

G. His music is characterized by contrapuntal excellence, formal innovations and religious idealism. He resembled Johann Sebastian Bach in his singleness of purpose and loftiness of ideals. His themes are apt to center around a pivotal note; he often begins a movement or section with a short figure which is repeated two or three times. He shows a fondness for keys with many sharps, seeming to attach a mystic significance to their use. He makes frequent use of a modulatory scheme with roots dropping a third and basses moving in chromatic lines. Cyclic form and the use of canons are characteristic.

H. The Schola Cantorum (founded in 1894 by Alexandre Guilmant, d'Indy and Bordes) was organized to perpetuate Franck's influence and methods. After the death of d'Indy (1931), several members withdrew and began the École César Franck (1935).

III. Catalogue of Chamber Works

A. Trios for Piano, Violin, Cello (1840-1842)
   1. Op. 1, No. 1 in F-sharp minor; No. 2 in B-flat major; No. 3 in B minor
   2. Op. 2 in B minor
B. Quintet for Piano, 2 Violins, Viola, Cello in F minor (1878-1879)
C. Piano and Violin
   1. *Andante quietoso* in A major (1843)
   2. *Duo pour pianoforte et violon concertante* (on themes from Dalayrac's *Gulistan*) Op. 14 (1844)
   3. *Sonata* in A major (1886)
D. String Quartet in D major (1889)

IV. Trios for Piano, Violin, Cello

A. The first three trios were written in 1840 and published later as Op. 1. They were dedicated to Leopold I, King of Belgium, the presentation being made by the composer in person, but without any recorded reward. The influence of Beethoven is shown in Op. 1, No. 1; influence of Schubert and Weber in Nos. 2 and 3.

B. Trio Op. 1, No. 1 in F-sharp minor
   1. Cyclical form. Themes from the first movement are used again (somewhat transformed) in later movements. Other themes are derived from the main theme.
   2. Andante con moto (F-sharp minor)
      a. Two themes, one the countersubject to the other, are stated at the beginning (meas. 9) in the cello and piano. The countersubject (piano) was used more than thirty years later as the cyclic theme in the Quintet for Piano and Strings.
      b. A third theme (meas. 83) completes the melodic materials.
      c. The movement is in five sections; themes A and A^1 are treated in sections 1, 3, 4; theme B is merely stated (not developed) in sections 2 and 5.
   3. Allegro molto (B minor)
      a. A Scherzo with double repetition is followed (meas. 213) by the first Trio (B major), derived from the theme of the Scherzo itself. After the third section (a repetition of the first), a second Trio (being the expressive third theme from the first movement accompanied by a rhythmic bass derived from the Scherzo theme) is introduced (meas. 411; combined in meas. 472).

   b.   In the fifth section (meas. 539), the cyclic theme A^1 is combined with the Scherzo theme (meas. 557). The movement ends with an allusion to the second Trio and proceeds "attacca" to the Finale.
  4.   Allegro maestoso (F-sharp major)
   a.   The only movement in sonata-form. It is longer and more developed than the others. The opening phrase is a stirring version of the cyclic theme A. The second theme (D-flat major) is in Franck's religious mood. The movement follows regular formal lines, with the cyclic B theme triumphant at the end.
C. Trio No. 2 in B-flat major; Trio No. 3 in B minor
  1.   The works are inferior to the first Trio, both in material and musical interest.
  2.   Franck called No. 2 in B-flat major a "drawing-room trio."
D. Trio No. 4 in B minor (listed by Cobbett as B major)
  1.   Liszt, whom Franck met in Belgium, induced the rewriting of the final movement of the third Trio as a new, single-movement work. Franck therefore supplied a new finale for No. 3. It was published under the title of "Fourth Trio, Op. 2," and dedicated "To my friend Fr. Liszt."
  2.   The work is original in form. The Recapitulation begins with the second subject.

V.   **Quintet in F minor for Piano, Two Violins, Viola, Cello** (*M* 1, p. 141)

A.   First performed in 1880 at the Société Nationale de Musique. One of the most popular of all piano quintets. In it the cyclic principle is carried to extreme limits.
B.   In the interval between the early chamber works and the Quintet (almost forty years), Franck slowly developed his unique harmonic style, with rich modulations and "chromatic wandering" as marked characteristics.   The result was a type of writing best described as "restless and colorful, but showing a somewhat loose harmonic structure." The Quintet is an example of this, at the same time demonstrating great economy of thematic resources.
C.   An expressive melody (cyclical theme of the entire piece) is used, in various forms, as the second theme and the Coda of the first movement, in the Development of the slow movement, and as the theme of the Finale's extended Coda. Each time it is altered in rhythm and tempo. This important theme was in turn derived from one of the cyclical themes of the Trio No. 1 in F-sharp minor.
D.   The theme transformations are accompanied by sudden changes of mood and tempo, with modulations often being to remote keys (first movement in F minor presents the cyclical theme in the keys of E major, G major, F-sharp minor, A major, D-flat major). Tempo and dynamic changes of "molto ritardando" and "molto crescendo" are indicated.
E.   Each of the three movements is in sonata-form, with an Exposition, Development and Recapitulation. In addition, the first and final movements have Introductions and elaborate Codas. Characteristics of the Franck style, however, make the music seem somewhat episodical.
F.   Molto moderato quasi lento - Maestoso - Allegro (F minor)
  1.   The movement is built on two themes. After an introduction and statement of the first theme (meas. 50), which is derived from the opening phrase, a cyclic melody appears in several exploratory keys and is then finally announced in A-flat major (meas. 124), thus taking the function of a second subject. This second element is important in the Development (meas. 143-269), appears in the Recapitulation (meas. 269-350), and in the Coda (meas. 350-440).
G.   Lento, con molto sentimento (A minor)
  1.   Three themes are used in the three sections of the movement: 1) the opening lento theme, which is heard in the first violin, then in other strings, and finally in the piano; 2) the cyclic theme of the Quintet (this time in D-flat, piano part, meas. 58); 3) a

melodic element which appears only during the Exposition of the movement (meas. 20), but reappears in the final movement as a second subject.

H. Allegro non troppo, ma con fuoco (F major)
   1. A movement of great brilliance. It opens with an Introduction based on fragments of the material to follow. The first subject is fully announced by unison strings (meas. 73) and is followed (after a bridge passage built on fragments of the same melodic element) by the second theme (piano, meas. 147), which is derived from the second movement. The Development is built on the two themes. The first is treated rhythmically, the second is developed chromatically. At the end of the Recapitulation the cyclic theme is heard again (by augmentation and change of rhythm, meas. 388 in D-flat major; meas. 404 in F minor in combination with the first subject). A fast-moving Coda (meas. 430) closes the movement and the work.

VI. **Quartet in D major for Two Violins, Viola, Cello** (1889) (*M* 1, p. 125)

A. The last of Franck's chamber compositions. It was written only a few months before his death, and the first performance took place April 19, 1890, at the Société Nationale de Musique.

B. Like the Quintet, the Symphony in D minor and the Violin Sonata in A major, this work is based on a generating theme which supplies the complete musical material. It is one of Franck's finest compositions and a high point in nineteenth century French music, if judged for technical mastery, nobility of conception and wealth of color. The idea of cyclical form is employed probably more consistently than in any chamber music work since Beethoven.

C. Poco lento - Allegro (D major - D minor - D major)
   1. This movement combines two separate musical forms (each individual and complete) so that the effect is one of a sonata-form inscribed within an A - B - A form. The Exposition of the A - B - A in slow time is constructed of the "germ motif" (meas. 1-6). The sonata Exposition follows at once, with the two transitional themes: A in D minor (meas. 61), B in F major (meas. 138). These two themes are connected by an important cyclic figure (cello, meas. 105-106) which is much used in the Finale. At this point the second part of the A - B - A appears (in place of the usual Development of the sonata themes), in the form of fugal entries of the original lento element (meas. 174). Development (meas. 218), Recapitulation (meas. 271) of the sonata Exposition. The final section of the A - B - A pattern follows (meas. 340).

D. Scherzo (F-sharp minor - F-sharp major)
   1. Characterized by feathery lightness; the use of mutes, and many measures of silence. There is a short quotation of the song-form of the first movement (cello, meas. 225), after which the Scherzo is resumed.

E. Larghetto (B major)
   1. Less organic connection with the other movements. Extended aria form in five sections: A - B - A - C - A. The fourth section contains references to the Trio material in the preceding movement.

F. Allegro molto - Larghetto - Allegro molto - Vivace (D major)
   1. Sonata-form. Begins with an Introduction which reviews themes of the previous movements. The original "cyclic theme" of the first movement is finally given a place of importance.
   2. The Finale actually begins in measure 59. The A theme of the Exposition uses the opening of the "cyclic theme." The B part of the Exposition is a re-use of the bridge motif found in the Exposition of the first movement.
      a. This latter element is very important in the Development of the final movement. It is found in augmentation (meas. 113); then as adapted for a second subject in double augmentation (meas. 137). In this final form, it is a complete theme of three

distinct parts (beginning meas. 137, meas. 193, meas. 237). Frequent changes of tempo and mood, added to a wealth of color achieved by modulations to remote keys, make this movement a striking one, a magnificent conclusion to the chamber music of César Franck.

SELECTED BIBLIOGRAPHY

Books

1. Andriessen, Hendrik. *César Franck*, tr. Walter Alfred George Doyle-Davidson. Stockholm: The Continental Book Co., 1947.
2. Davies, Laurence. *César Franck and His Circle*. Boston: Houghton Mifflin, 1970.
3. Demuth, Norman. *César Franck*. New York: Philosophical Library, 1949.
4. Gallois, Jean. *Franck*. Paris: Éditions du Seuil, 1966.
5. d'Indy, Vincent. *César Franck*, tr. Rosa Newmarch. New York: Dover Publications, 1965. (reprint of 1910 edition) (Quartet: pp. 182-197)
6. Vallas, Léon. *César Franck*, tr. Hubert J. Foss. New York: Oxford University Press, 1951.

Articles

1. Frank, Paul L. "The Cyclic Principle as Used by César Franck and Anton Bruckner." *JAMS* 12 (1959), pp. 98-99.
2. Roberts, W. Wright. "César Franck." *ML* 3 (1922), pp. 317-328.

Music

Study (Miniature) Scores

1. *Miscellaneous Chamber Works,* ed. Albert E. Wier. New York: Melville, NY: Belwin-Mills, 1973.
2. String Quartet in D major: *EE* 323.
3. Piano Trio, Op. 1, No. 1: *EE* 360.
4. Piano Quintet in F minor: *EE* 329.

Playing Parts and Scores

5. String Quartet in D major: *PE* 3746.
6. Piano Trio, Op. 1, No. 1: *PE* 3745; New York: International Music Company, 1943.
7. Piano Quintet in F minor: *PE* 3743; Paris: Hamelle, 188-.
8. Sonata in A major for Violin and Piano: *PE* 3742.

OUTLINE XII

GABRIEL-URBAIN FAURÉ (1845 - 1924)

I. Life

1845   Born in Pamiers, Ariège, May 12.

1856   Studied at the "École de Musique religieuse" with Louis Niedermeyer, also with Pierre Dietsch and Camille Saint-Saëns.

1866   Organist at Saint-Sauveur in Rennes.

1870   Assistant organist at Saint-Sulpice and organist at Saint-Honoré d'Eylau in Paris.

1896   Organist at the Madeleine. Succeeded Jules Massenet as professor of composition, counterpoint and fugue at the Conservatoire. Became known as a song composer.

1905   Succeeded Théodore Dubois as director of the Conservatoire (retired in 1920).

1924   Died in Paris, November 4.

II. Catalogue of Chamber Music

A. One String Quartet, Op. 121 in E minor (1924)

B. Two Piano Quintets, Op. 89 in D minor (1906), Op. 115 in C minor (1921)

C. Two Piano Quartets, Op. 15 in C minor (1879), Op. 45 in G minor (1886)

D. One Trio for Piano, Violin, Cello, Op. 120 in D minor (1923)

E. Two Sonatas for Violin, Piano, Op. 13 in A major (1876), Op. 108 in E minor (1917)

F. Two Sonatas for Cello, Piano, Op. 109 in D minor (1918), Op. 117 in G minor (1922)

III. Style

A. Fauré occupies a unique place in the musical life of his native France. He was one of the first to break away from the romantic school with its restricted harmonic idiom, and pointed the way toward greater harmonic freedom by the use of medieval modes. He represents the maturity of French chamber music and he influenced many French composers. Among his pupils were Charles Kœchlin, Georges Enesco, Florent Schmitt, Maurice Ravel, Nadia Boulanger, Raoul Laparra and Jean Jules Roger-Ducasse. Fauré is probably best known through his songs. His chamber works constitute less than one tenth of his total output of over 130 works, but they are an important contribution.

B. Fauré represents a new post-romantic French style with some suggestions of the coming impressionism. His style is fluent, reflective, controlled, sensitive, elegant. He used augmented triads, chords of the seventh, ninth, eleventh and thirteenth; appoggiaturas; parallelism (planing); syncopation; whole-tone scales; irregular resolutions of dissonances. Other characteristics of his style are the use of non-chordal tones in the bass, free treatment of inversions, rapid return to the key at a cadence.

C. His chamber music may be divided into the usual three periods. These periods are not based on radical differences in styles, but on the growth of the composer in freedom from influences of forerunners such as Charles Gounod and Camille Saint-Saëns. The stylistic periods are also indicated by an ever increasing evidence of his own individuality as expressed especially through harmonic and melodic idioms and rhythmic unity.

1. First period (1876-1886) includes: Sonata for Violin and Piano, Op. 13; two Piano Quartets, Op. 15 and Op. 45.

2. Second period (1906-1921) includes: Piano Quintet, Op. 89 (announced earlier as Op. 60); Piano Quintet, Op. 115.

3. Third period (1922-1924) includes: Sonata for Cello and Piano, Op. 117; String

Quartet, Op. 121.

IV. Chamber Music

A. Piano Quartet, Op. 15 in C minor for Violin, Viola, Cello, Piano (1879) (*M* 1, p. 103)
1. Allegro molto moderato (C minor)
   a. The quartet opens with a clean-cut, rhythmic theme. The three strings, in their best range, are supported by the piano with syncopated chords. Through a series of enharmonic changes the second theme is arrived at in E-flat major (meas. 37).
2. Allegro vivo (E-flat major)
   a. This Scherzo is a masterpiece of balance between piano and strings. Use of staccato, pizzicato, syncopated rhythms and the characteristic interval of the augmented fourth.
3. Adagio (C minor)
   a. The opening theme in the cello is answered by a theme in A-flat major in the first violin (meas. 27) which is reminiscent of Schumann.
4. Allegro molto (C minor)
   a. The Finale begins with mazurka-like rhythms with occasional measures in four-beat meter. There are three themes: 1) strong, rhythmic (meas. 2); 2) lyrical (meas. 95); 3) based on a rhythmic pattern found in the Exposition (meas. 149).
B. Piano Quartet, Op. 45 in G minor for Violin, Viola, Cello, Piano (1886)
1. There are four movements, paralleling in construction and order of sequence those of the earlier Piano Quartet, Op. 15. This work shows a marked growth in the mastery of workmanship and in the individuality of the composer. The Scherzo has the only use of the cyclic form to be found in his chamber music.
2. The strong impassioned opening theme is followed by a graceful second theme, which appears after being interrupted in its entrance by the main theme. A quiet third theme follows.
3. Allegro molto (C minor)
   a. The Scherzo begins with a pizzicato accompaniment figure in the strings. Both themes of the first movement are then used with a change from binary to ternary rhythm.
4. Adagio non troppo (G minor)
   a. Outstanding in rhythmic and melodic invention. The tonality wavers between E-flat major and G minor. A bell-like effect appears in the fifths first sounded by the piano and later in the strings. The movement closes with the distant effect of muted strings.
5. Allegro molto (G minor)
   a. The Finale is characterized by a marked conflict between the themes. The rhythm, in triplet patterns, is first announced by the piano, then by the violin and viola. The movement ends with the themes in close stretto.
C. Piano Quintet, Op. 89 in D minor for Two Violins, Viola, Cello, Piano (1906)
1. Allegro moderato (D minor)
   a. The three themes of this movement are used with skill, although the quintet as a whole is not one of Fauré's best chamber works.
2. Adagio (G minor)
   a. Based on two themes. The first is in G minor in 12/8, stated by strings with the piano in triplets. The second is in B minor in 4/4 and treated canonically. There is some use of chromaticism.
3. Allegretto moderato (D major)
   a. A scherzo-like movement. The theme in D major is derived from a part of the first theme of the first movement. This is contrasted with a quieter theme in B minor. The form suggests a Rondo.

D. Piano Quintet, Op. 115 in C minor for Two Violins, Viola, Cello, Piano (1921)
   1. Allegro moderato (C minor)
      a. The opening theme is stated by the viola after one measure of an arpeggiated figure in the piano. This is taken up by the other strings; cello, second violin (E-flat major), first violin (C minor). The second theme is given out by the strings in the form of chords.
      b. The Development involves canonic imitation between the strings and the piano. In the Coda an unusual harmonic effect is obtained by the alternation of the tonic chord (now in C major) in its first inversion with it in root position as a tonic seventh chord.
   2. Allegro vivo (E-flat major)
      a. The Scherzo is used for the first time since the Piano Quartet, Op. 45. There is an unusual alteration of scale passages throughout the movement. At the beginning the piano announces a scale on E-flat which has a raised fourth degree, and also a passing chromatic C-sharp. In the third measure a Phrygian scale is used on E-flat. Modal treatment is used extensively.
   3. Andante moderato (G major)
      a. The first theme is announced by the strings. The second theme is in the piano with a counter-theme in the upper strings as a descending scale in G major.
   4. Allegro molto (C minor)
      a. The viola announces the first theme in two two-measure phrases. It then appears in immediate succession in the second violin, then in the first violin. The piano meanwhile supplies a bass which is accented in duple meter. The movement concludes in C major with a very long passage in stretto.
E. Trio, Op. 120 in D minor for Piano, Violin, Cello (1923)
   1. Allegro ma non troppo (D minor)
      a. The opening theme is given out by the cello. Use is made of the characteristic interval of the fourth. The texture is thin and the melodies are simple, yet the effect is strong. Some use is made of the Lydian mode.
   2. Andantino (F major)
      a. This fine movement is characterized by an expressive theme opening in the Lydian mode.
   3. Allegro vivo (D minor)
      a. Modulates through foreign keys without destroying the essential tonality.
F. String Quartet, Op. 121 in E minor (1924)
   1. Allegro moderato (E minor)
      a. Fauré's last work begins in a serious and melancholy vein and maintains an evenness of texture with little variety. The second theme enters in measure 35 and the Recapitulation in measure 111.
   2. Andante (A minor)
      a. This movement begins with a somber theme in the Locrian mode. Syncopation characterizes the rhythmic patterns.
   3. Allegro (E minor - E major)
      a. Rondo form: A - B - A - C - B - A - B - A
      b. A (meas. 1-41) - B (meas. 41-78) - A (meas. 79-116) - C (meas. 117-141) - B (meas. 142-163) - A (meas. 163-234) - B (meas. 234-260) - A (meas. 260-301) - Coda (meas. 302-312).

SELECTED BIBLIOGRAPHY

Books

1. Kœchlin, Charles. *Gabriel Fauré (1845-1924)*, tr. Leslie Orrey. London: Dennis Dobson, 1946. (Chamber Music: pp. 40-46)
2. Suckling, Norman. *Fauré*. New York: E. P. Dutton, 1951. (Chamber Music: pp. 90-119)
3. Vuillermoz, Émile. *Gabriel Fauré*, tr. Kenneth Schapin. Philadelphia: Chilton, 1969.

Articles

1. Beechey, Gwilym E. "The Violin Sonatas of Gabriel Fauré." *Strad* 86 (Dec 1975), p. 559.
2. –––––––"The Cello Sonatas of Gabriel Fauré." *Strad* 88 (Jun 1977), p. 151.
3. Chandler, T. "Gabriel Fauré, A Re-appraisal." *MM* 22 (1945), p. 165.
4. Coeury, A. "Gabriel Fauré." *Sackbut* 5 (Mar 1925), p. 235.
5. Copland, Aaron. "Gabriel Fauré, A Neglected Master." *MQ* 10 (1924), pp. 573-586.
6. Landormy, Paul. "Gabriel Fauré." *MQ* 17 (1931), pp. 293-301.
7. Orrey, Leslie. "Gabriel Fauré, 1845-1924." *MT* 86 (1945), p. 137.
8. Suckling, Norman. "Gabriel Fauré, Classic of Modern Times." *MR* 6 (1945), pp. 65-71.

Music

Study (Miniature) Scores

1. *Miscellaneous Chamber Works*, ed. Albert E. Wier. Melville, NY: Belwin-Mills, 1973.
2. *Quatuor à cordes*, Op. 121. Paris: Durand, 1925.
3. Piano Quartets, Op. 15, 45: *EE*.

Playing Parts and Scores

4. *Quatuor à cordes*, Op. 121. Paris: Durand, 1925; Philadelphia: Elkan-Vogel, 1925.
5. Piano Trio in D minor, Op. 120. Paris: Durand, 1966.
6. Piano Quartet in C minor, Op. 15. New York: International Music Company, 1945.
7. Piano Quartet in G minor, Op. 45. New York: International Music Company, 1950.
8. Piano Quintet in D minor, Op. 89. New York: G. Schirmer, 1907.
9. Piano Quintet in C minor, Op. 115. Paris: Durand, 1921; Philadelphia: Elkan-Vogel, 1921.
10. Sonata for Violin and Piano, Op. 13. Wiesbaden: Breitkopf & Härtel. (*BH* 2569) ·
11. Sonata for Violin and Piano, Op. 108. Paris: Durand, 1966; Philadelphia: Elkan-Vogel, 1966.
12. Sonata for Cello and Piano, Op. 109. Paris: Durand, 1968; Philadelphia: Elkan-Vogel, 1968.
13. Sonata for Cello and Piano, Op. 117. Paris: Durand, 1922; Philadelphia: Elkan-Vogel, 1922.

OUTLINE XIII

(ACHILLE-) CLAUDE DEBUSSY (1862 - 1918)

I.   Life

1862   Born in Saint-Germain-en-Laye, August 22.

1873   Entered the Conservatoire in Paris after studies with Mme. Mauté de Fleurville, a pupil of Chopin. Studied piano with Antoine François Marmontel, solfeggio with Albert Lavignac, harmony with Émile Durand.

1880   Met Tschaikowsky's patroness, Mme. Nadezhda von Meck and travelled with her in Italy, Switzerland, Austria and Russia. Influenced by Mme. Vasnier, a singer, to whom he dedicated *Fêtes galantes* on poems by Paul Verlaine.

1884   Won the *Grand Prix de Rome* with his cantata *L'Enfant prodigue*. Wrote *La Damoiselle élue* (1887).

1892   Wrote *L'Après-midi d'un faune*; began *Pelléas et Mélisande*; *Premier Quatuor* (1893).

1901   *Trois Nocturnes* (*Nuages, Fêtes, Sirènes*) dedicated to his first wife Rosalie Texier (married 1899). In 1904 he married Mme. Emma Bardac.

1905   *La Mer* completed in March in England. *Images* (1906).

1908   Conducted his own works in London, Paris, Vienna, Budapest, Turin, Moscow, St. Petersburg, The Hague and Rome.

1914   Planned an American tour with the violinist Arthur Hartmann, but gave it up because of ill health.

1918   Died in Paris, March 25, of cancer.

II.   Catalogue of Chamber Music

A.   String Quartet, Op. 10 in G minor (1893)
B.   Rhapsody for Saxophone and Piano (1903-1905)
C.   First Rhapsody for Clarinet and Piano (1909-1910)
D.   Sonata for Violoncello in D minor (1915)
E.   Sonata for Flute (or Violin), Viola, Harp in G minor (1916)
F.   Sonata for Violin and Piano in G minor - G major (1916-1917)

III.   Style

A.   Debussy developed a new style in music known as "Impressionism." It began as a revolt against dynamic, logical German classicism and the extravagant emotionalism of romanticism. Paintings of the French Impressionists Claude Monet and Pierre Auguste Renoir, and the refined poetry of Paul Verlaine (1844-1896), Stéphane Mallarmé and others suggested a new type of music, essentially French in nature.

B.   Although the first great composer of "New Music" of the twentieth century, Debussy is sometimes said to represent the final culmination of romanticism. His musical style was evolved from elements found in the music of César Franck, Richard Wagner (whose music he disliked), Alexander Borodin and Modest Moussorgsky. He was also influenced by the delicacy and poetry of Frederic Chopin and the rhythms and colors of Javanese music.

C.   Impressionism is concerned with sonority; the play of tone colors; transitory impressions and sensations; the veiled rather than the obvious; the translation of poetry into music; unusual and striking instrumental colors and harmonies; form based on the mood and color of the sections.

D. Characteristics of harmonic style
   1. Usually there is one principal part, which is colored by chords; real part-writing is rarely if ever used.
   2. Chords in parallel motion (parallelism, "planing").
   3. Melodic lines are short and are often used as motives.
   4. Whole-tone and pentatonic scales are sometimes used in melodies and chordal combinations, including tritones and augmented intervals. Chromatic lines are used for special effects.
   5. Modes are used; sometimes one mode is used melodically while another is used harmonically (major, minor or church modes).
   6. Frequent use of common chords in unusual successions; seventh chords and triads; triads with added seconds, fourths, sixths and sevenths; augmented fourths.
   7. Unresolved dissonances. Freedom in modulations, often enharmonic.
   8. Key changes of a third, second or fifth relationships. Rapid changes in harmony occur.

IV. Chamber Music

A. Premier Quatuor, Op. 10 in G minor (1893) (*M* 1, p. 21)
   1. Chamber music represents only a small part of Debussy's compositions. His first chamber music work, the Quartet, does not break completely with the past, but the general effect is entirely unlike other music. There is some use of the principles of development; repetition; a little imitation; sequence modulations; rhythmic transformations; cyclic treatment. About one-half of the chords are sevenths, over one-third are triads. Most of the remaining are ninth chords, with a very few eleventh and thirteenth chords. Seventh chords often have the close (dissonant) intervals at the bottom, which accentuates the dissonance. The seventh is approached and left freely.
   2. Animé et très décidé (G minor)
      a. Sonata-form with more than the usual number of themes. The generating theme A, in Phrygian mode, appears frequently throughout the movement, somewhat like a Wagnerian *leitmotiv*.
      b. Exposition: A - B (meas. 13) - A (meas. 26) - C (second theme, meas. 39) - D (meas. 51).
      c. Development: A (meas. 61) - E (sometimes called the second theme, meas. 63) - A - E - A - E - A.
      d. Recapitulation: A (meas. 138) - F (meas. 149) - E (meas. 161) - G (meas. 169) - E (meas. 175) - Coda (meas. 183).
   3. Assez vif et bien rhythmé (G major)
      a. The form is basically A - B - A - B (developed) - Coda. The material is mostly derived from the generating theme A. Much use of pizzicato.
      b. The generating theme A is presented in a Scherzo mood by the viola (meas. 3) with many repetitions. A subsidiary theme appears in the first violin (meas. 9). Theme A is in the first violin (meas. 37) and cello (meas. 47).
      c. Theme B (second theme) is an augmentation of theme A (meas. 56).
      d. Theme A is in the viola (meas. 86), the second violin (meas. 94), the first violin (meas. 100).
      e. Theme B (meas. 111) is developed with altered rhythms and varied tonalities.
      f. The Coda (15/8 time) begins with a modified version of the A theme in the viola (meas. 148). It concludes (meas. 168) with the tremolo figure used to introduce the B theme (meas. 54).
   4. Andantino, doucement expressif (D-flat major)
      a. The generating theme A is only remotely connected, if at all, with this movement. The lyrical feeling in the melody recalls the slow movement of Borodin's First Symphony.

b. Form: A - B - C (developed) - B - A. The relation of the C theme to the B theme results in a feeling of ternary form.

c. Theme A appears after the "motto" beginning (meas. 1-4). Mutes are used in all four instruments. Characteristic Debussy harmonies are found in measure 15.

d. The second section (meas. 28) is introduced by theme B (or second theme) in the viola, which is varied in the following measure.

e. Theme C, an extension of theme B, enters in the viola (meas. 48). This theme then appears in the cello (meas. 55); in octaves with the cello and second violin (meas. 62). The use of a whole-tone scale (accompanied by thirds), and the resulting augmented triads, is characteristic of many later works. The climax of the movement is reached in measures 76-79. The Development of theme C continues with the use of part of the theme, repetition and sequence. The last statement of the first part of the theme in solo cello (meas. 91) is introduced by a whole-tone scale.

f. Theme B returns, stated in octaves (meas. 95), and the solo cello modulates back to theme A.

5. Très modéré (D-flat major - G major)

 a. Form: Introduction - A - B - A - C - Coda. Theme C is the generating theme.

 b. Introduction (meas. 1-30). Theme C is used in altered form and appears in imitation (meas. 15-20). The theme is divided between the cello and viola (meas. 21-24) and then appears in octaves between the viola and the first violin, accompanied by the second violin and cello in octaves (meas. 25-26). The Introduction ends at measure 30.

 c. The Finale actually begins with the Très mouvementé (meas. 31). The A theme is in the viola (meas. 31-32). There is a suggestion of the generating theme C in the first and second violins (meas. 45-53). Theme A returns in measures 55-56.

 d. Theme B is derived from the second measure of theme A. Theme B is divided between the violin and viola (meas. 59-60). It is used in sequence and as a repeated rhythmic figure in the viola. It then appears in the first violin (meas. 69). The transition to theme A (meas. 91-113) uses fragments of the A theme in augmentation in the cello (meas. 98), and in octaves between the cello and violin (meas. 106-109). The second measure of theme A is altered and in augmentation (meas. 110-113). Theme A is in octaves, accompanied by chromatic lines in octaves (meas. 114-118).

 e. Theme C (second theme), the generating theme, is used in augmentation, accompanied by a rhythmic ostinato from theme A (meas. 125); in augmentation and syncopated (meas. 141); in a triplet figure in the viola (meas. 145) and later in the second violin. Theme A in the first violin is combined with the augmented theme C in the second violin (meas. 166-170), then in the second violin and viola (meas. 181) and extended.

 f. Theme A appears again (meas. 216) and the two parts of theme A are used in various ways. Theme B is used in augmentation in the cello (meas. 232-236). Theme A is in octaves (meas. 241). The second part of theme A appears in augmentation (meas. 242-243).

 g. Theme C is varied in the second violin and viola (meas. 244). There is some use of imitation (meas. 248-251). Themes C, A and B are varied (meas. 252-287). Theme C is in augmentation in the second violin (meas. 289) and extended in the first violin (meas. 298).

 h. The Coda (meas. 325) is based on generating theme C as it appears in the Scherzo movement. Theme B is in the cello (meas. 333). The triplet figure of the theme (meas. 348) leads to a brilliant conclusion.

B. Sonata for Flute (Violin), Viola, Harp in G minor (1916)

 1. Pastorale, Interlude, Finale. The themes of the movements are all closely related. The entire work is rhythmically complex.

 2. The form of the first movement is ternary. There are five short, arabesque-like themes

and polytonality is suggested. The bright Interlude is marked "Tempo di Minuetto" and the last movement is rapid and rhythmic.

SELECTED BIBLIOGRAPHY

Books

1. Calvocoressi, Michel Dimitri. *Debussy*. London: Novello & Co., 1944.
2. Debussy, Claude. *Debussy on Music*, tr. Richard L. Smith. New York: Alfred A. Knopf, 1977.
3. –––––––*Monsieur Croche, the Dilettante Hater*, tr. B. N. Langdon Davies. New York: Lear Publishers, 1948.
4. Dumesnil, Maurice. *Claude Debussy, Master of Dreams*. New York: Ives Washburn, 1940.
5. –––––––*How to Play and Teach Debussy*. New York: Schroeder & Gunther, 1932.
6. Harvey, Harry B. *Claude of France, the Story of Debussy*. New York: Allen, Towne and Heath, 1948.
7. Jarociński, Stefan. *Debussy: Impressionism and Symbolism*, tr. Rollo Myers. London: Eulenberg Books, 1976.
8. Lockspeiser, Edward. *Debussy*. London: J. M. Dent, 1951; New York: Pellegrini and Cudahy, 1951. (Chamber Music: pp. 163-181)
9. –––––––*Debussy; His Life and Mind*, Vol. I, 1862-1902. New York: Macmillan, 1962.
10. –––––––*Debussy; His Life and Mind*, Vol. II, 1902-1918. New York: Macmillan, 1965.
11. Ketting, Pier. *Claude-Achille Debussy*, tr. Walter Doyle-Davidson. Stockholm: Continental Book Co., 1947.
12. Mason, Daniel Gregory. *Contemporary Composers*, Chapter IV. New York: Macmillan, 1918.
13. Shera, Franck Henry. *Debussy and Ravel*. New York: Oxford University Press, 1927.
14. Thompson, Oscar. *Debussy, Man and Artist*. New York: Tudor Publishing Co., 1940. (reprint: New York: Dover Publications, 1967)
15. Vallas, Léon. *Claude Debussy, His Life and Works*, tr. Maire and Grace O'Brien. New York: Oxford University Press, 1933. (reprint: New York: Dover Publications, 1973)
16. –––––––*The Theories of Claude Debussy*, tr. Maire O'Brien. New York: Oxford University Press, 1929. (reprint: New York: Dover Publications, 1967)

Articles

1. Bauer, Harold. "Recollections of Debussy." *Musician* 36 (Feb 1931), p. 21.
2. Cross, Anthony. "Debussy and Bartók." *MT* 108 (1967), pp. 125-127.
3. Dumesnil, Maurice. "Claude Debussy as a Music Critic." *Etude* 64 (Apr 1946), p. 203.
4. Franco, Johan. "Debussy as a Melodist." *MA* 60 (Nov. 25, 1940), p. 5.
5. Howat, Roy. "Debussy, Ravel and Bartók; Towards Some New Concepts of Form." *ML* 58 (1977), pp. 285-293.
6. Lavauden, Thérèse. "Humour in the Work of Debussy." *Chesterian* 9 (1928), pp. 183, 209.
7. Lesuré, François. "Claude Debussy after His Centennary." *MQ* 49 (1963), pp. 277-288.
8. Lockspeiser, Edward. "Debussy During the Last War." *MA* 61 (Feb 10, 1941), p. 227.
9. –––––––"New Literature on Debussy." *ML* 40 (1959), pp. 140-149.
10. –––––––"Some Projects of Debussy." *Chesterian* 17 (1935), p. 11.
11. Mellers, Wilfrid H. "The Final Works of Claude Debussy." *ML* 20 (1939), pp. 168-176.
12. Moevs, Robert. "Intervallic Procedures in Debussy: Serenade from the Sonata for Cello and Piano, 1915." *PNM* 8 (Fall-Winter 1969), pp. 82-101.
13. Molié, Denyse. "Apropos of the Interpretation of Claude Debussy." *Eolus* 8 (1928), p. 13.

14. Myers, Rollo Hugh. "Claude Debussy and Russian Music." *ML* 39 (1958), pp. 336-342.
15. Palache, John G. "Debussy as Critic." *MQ* 10 (1924), pp. 361-368.
16. Phillips, C. Henry. "The Symbolists and Debussy." *ML* 13 (1932), pp. 298-311.
17. *Revue Musicale, La* 1 (Dec 1920), entire issue devoted to Debussy (in French).
18. Sabaneyev, Leonid L. "Claude Debussy." *ML* 10 (1929), pp. 1-34.
19. Ternant, Andrew de. "Debussy and Brahms." *MT* 65 (1924), p. 608.

Music

Study (Miniature) Scores

1. String Quartet, Op. 10: *EE* 210; *IMC*.

Playing Parts and Scores

2. String Quartet, Op. 10. New York: International Music Company, 1950.
3. *Sonate pour violoncello et piano*. Paris: Durand, 1965; Philadelphia: Elkan-Vogel, 1965; *PE* 9122.
4. *Sonate pour flûte, alto et harpe*. Paris: Durand, 1961; Philadelphia: Elkan-Vogel, 1961.
5. *Sonate pour violon et piano*. Paris: Durand, 1965; Philadelphia: Elkan-Vogel, 1965; *PE* 9121.

OUTLINE XIV

(JOSEPH) MAURICE RAVEL (1875 - 1937)

I. Life

1875   Born in Ciboure, Basses-Pyrénées, March 7. His family moved to Paris when he was three months old. He studied piano with Henri Ghis (1882) and later, harmony with Charles René.

1889   Entered the Conservatoire, where he studied with Charles de Bériot and Émile Pessard. He began to compose and became a pupil of Gabriel Fauré (1897) and André Gédalge. His artistic personality was revealed in his first works.

1899   Made his debut as conductor. He won the second *Prix de Rome* (1901) with his cantata *Myrrha*, but failed to win first prize in three attempts.

1905   In spite of academic hostility and the accusation that he imitated Debussy, Ravel continued to compose in his own highly individualistic manner. *Daphnis et Chloé* (1909-1911) definitely established his reputation.

1916   Drove an ambulance at the front during World War I (1916-1917). Appeared as pianist and conductor and was in the United States and Canada (1928). Received a Doctor of Music degree from Oxford University (1928), but refused the Legion of Honor. Ralph Vaughan Williams was one of his few pupils.

1930   Last important compositions were two piano concertos, one for left hand alone (1930-1931). He suffered from a cerebral disorder and was unable to compose after 1933.

1937   Died in Paris, December 28.

II. Catalogue of Chamber Music

A.   Quartet in F major (1902)
B.   Introduction and Allegro for Harp solo, Flute, Clarinet, String Quartet (1906)
C.   Three Poems of Stéphane Mallarmé for Voice, Piccolo, Flute, Two Clarinets, String Quartet (1913)
   1.   *Soupir*
   2.   *Placet futile*
   3.   *Surgi de la croupe et du bond*
D.   Trio in A minor for Violin, Cello, Piano (1915)
E.   Sonata for Violin, Cello (1920-1922)
F.   Berceuse on the name of Fauré for Violin, Piano (1922)
G.   Sonata for Violin, Piano (1923-1927)
H.   *Chansons madécasses*
   1.   *Nahandève*
   2.   *Aoua!*
   3.   *Il est doux*

III. Style

A.   Ravel was influenced during his early years by Spanish and Russian (Rimsky-Korsakow) music, and later by his French contemporaries Erik Satie (opposed to Wagnerian style), Emmanuel Chabrier (lively melodies and rhythms, clear orchestration) and Saint-Saëns.

B.   His melodic lines are clear and sometimes modal. There is much use of seventh, eleventh and thirteenth chords; small intervals, bold harmonies; unresolved dissonances; nonhar-

93

SALEM COLLEGE SCHOOL OF MUSIC

monic tones; many appoggiaturas instead of traditional resolutions.

    1.   Long pedals, sometimes inverted, are used. Tonality is retained, although it may be modal or even polymodal. Modal melodies usually have a major harmonic background.

    2.   The whole-tone scale and chromatic progressions are avoided.

C.   Rhythms are subtle, bright, frequently changing, but rarely complicated. They are generally strong and straightforward in comparison with many of his contemporaries.

    1.   Ravel does not sacrifice clarity of outline for "impressionistic" effects, and the development of the poetic idea is the first consideration.

D.   Form follows the classical conception. Cyclic treatment is found in almost all works. The scoring is clean and colorful and very resonant considering the small groups employed. There is frequent repetition of phrases.

E.   Ravel's music is sensitive and colorfully and carefully designed. It is never sentimental.

    1.   Although considered to be a follower of Debussy, Ravel has a style which is original and individual. General similarities in the quartets of Ravel and Debussy include cyclic treatment, use of pizzicato in the second movement and mutes in the third movement. The two composers are, however, different as regards materials and methods.

IV. **Quartet in F major (1902).** Dedicated to Gabriel Fauré.

A.   The entire quartet shows great originality, and mature technique in handling and exploiting both melodic line and harmonic progression. It is never contrapuntal in the imitative sense, but has contrasting melodic lines running simultaneously.

B.   Allegro Moderato Très doux (F major)

    1.   Sonata-form. The Exposition has the first theme in F major, the second in D minor (meas. 55). The Development (meas. 69) begins with the second part of the second theme in B-flat major. The first theme is varied in the second violin (meas. 72). The second part of the Development begins in measure 84. The Recapitulation (meas. 129) begins in F major, and after a number of tonality changes, the second theme appears in F major (meas. 184). Transition to the Coda (meas. 199).

    2.   Melodically the form is very clear. Harmonically the analysis is more complex because of numerous appoggiaturas and appearances of incomplete ninth and eleventh chords. These chords are often voiced with a close spacing between the middle voices. The chief melodic interest is carried either by the first violin or the viola, with an occasional appearance in the second violin. The use of tremolo is frequent throughout the entire quartet, and also the characteristic repetitions of short phrases.

C.   Assez vif - Très rythmé (A minor)

    1.   A scherzo movement with interesting use of pizzicato. It is based on two contrasting themes. The first theme is in the Aeolian mode. Second theme (meas. 13). There is much use of cross-rhythms. The Development uses both themes in various tonalities, with many rhythmic and tempo changes. The recapitulation of the first section begins at measure 150.

D.   Très lent (A minor - G-flat major)

    1.   In fantasy style. Three contrasting themes. The second theme (meas. 19) is related to the main theme of the first movement. There are many changes of tempo and meter; use of mutes. Arpeggios and tremolos are used as an accompaniment figure.

E.   Vif et agité (F major)

    1.   Form: A - B - C - A - B - A - C - B - C - A - Coda. The movement begins with a rapid 5/8 in unison. A 5/4 bridges this into the B theme (meas. 54) which, although written in 3/4, gives no feeling of bar lines. The B theme is based on the first theme of the first movement. Theme C (meas. 74) is derived from the second theme of the first movement.

V. **Introduction et Allegro in G-flat major (1908)**

A. Scored for harp solo, flute, clarinet and string quartet. The first theme (Introduction) is in parallel thirds between the flute and clarinet. The second theme is given to strings in three parallel octaves (meas. 3-6). The cello, in a slightly faster passage, introduces the third theme with an arpeggiated accompaniment for strings and winds.

B. In the Allegro, the harp develops the second theme without accompaniment by the other instruments. This is followed by a tutti statement of the same theme. The harp joins the group again and the theme alternates between the flute and clarinet. After a short harp cadenza, the flute and clarinet present a new theme (fifth theme) in octaves. The first theme returns in muted strings, followed by a slightly altered version of the second theme in the harp. A rhapsodic section, using the fifth theme, follows. The second theme joins it twenty measures after a harp cadenza. These themes work toward the most extensive harp cadenza of the piece. The second theme appears in the harp after the cadenza. Following the development of the second theme, the fifth theme returns and is built up to a brilliant conclusion.

VI. Trio in A minor for Violin, Cello, Piano (1915)

A. Modéré
1. The piano gives the first statement of the theme. The violin and cello then join, two octaves apart. The second theme is slower and contrasting.

B. Pantoum
1. The colors of the violin are exploited by the use of pizzicato, arco, harmonics and double stops, all in four measures. The piano takes an active part in the ensemble and is not an accompanying instrument. The piano exploits the Ravel characteristic of presenting a complete thematic exposition early in the composition.

C. Passacaille (Très large)
1. The piano presents the theme in the bass. The cello takes it next while the piano plays a single bass line against it. The violin then has the theme while the piano adds a fuller harmonic support. This complete process is repeated with still more voices until the climax is reached over a pedal point in the piano. There is a gradual reduction of parts to the end.

D. Finale
1. The entire movement is built on three thematic ideas which have closely associated rhythms.
2. The movement opens in a fast 5/4 with a cello tremolo under the arpeggiated harmonics of the violins. The piano gives the first statement of the theme.

SELECTED BIBLIOGRAPHY

Books

1. Brooks, Donald. *Five Great French Composers, Their Lives and Works*. London: Rockliff, 1946.
2. Davies, Laurence. *The Gallic Muse*. New York: Barnes, 1969.
3. Demuth, Norman. *Ravel*. London: J. M. Dent, 1956; New York: Farrar, Straus and Cudahy, 1956. (Chamber Music: pp. 123-157)
4. Goss, Madeleine. *Bolero, the Life of Maurice Ravel*. New York: Henry Holt, 1940.
5. Jankélévitch, Vladimir. *Ravel*, tr. Margaret Crosland. New York: Grove Press, 1959.
6. Manuel, Roland. *Maurice Ravel*, tr. Cynthia Jolly. London: Dennis Dobson, 1947.
7. Miller, Horace Alden. *New Harmonic Devices*. Boston: Oliver Ditson Co., 1930.
8. Myers, Rollo Hugh. *Ravel, Life and Works*. New York: Thomas Yoseloff, 1960.
9. Onnen, Frank. *Maurice Ravel*, tr. Walter A. G. Doyle-Davidson. Stockholm: Continental

Book Co., 1947.

10. Orenstein, Arbie. *Ravel, Man and Musician.* New York: Columbia University Press, 1975.
11. Seroff, Victor I. *Maurice Ravel.* New York: Henry Holt, 1953.
12. Shera, Frank Henry. *Debussy and Ravel.* New York: Oxford University Press, 1951.
13. Stuckenschmidt, Hans H. *Maurice Ravel: Variations on His Life and Works,* tr. Samuel R. Rosenbaum. Philadelphia: Chilton Book Co., 1968.

Articles

1. Brian, Havergal. "Maurice Ravel." *Mus Opinion* (Nov 1939).
2. Calvocoressi, Michel Dimitri. "When Ravel Composed to Order." *ML* 22 (1941), pp. 54-59.
3. –––––––"Maurice Ravel." *MT* 89 (1938), p. 22.
4. Casella, Alfredo. "Ravel's Harmony." *MT* 67 (1926), p. 124.
5. Cushing, Charles C. "Maurice Ravel: 1875-1937." *MM* 15 (1938), p. 140.
6. Goosens, Eugene. "The String Quartet Since Brahms." *ML* 3 (1922), pp. 335-348.
7. Hammond, Richard. "Maurice Ravel, 1927." *MM* 5 (1928), p. 20.
8. Hill, Edward Burlingame. "Maurice Ravel." *MQ* 13 (1927), pp. 130-146.
9. Howat, Roy. "Debussy, Ravel and Bartók: Toward Some New Concepts of Form." *ML* 58 (1977), pp. 285-293.
10. Landormy, Paul. "Maurice Ravel." *MQ* 25 (1939), pp. 430-441.
11. Lockspeiser, Edward. "Roussel and Ravel." *ML* 19 (1938), pp. 245-250.
12. Morris, Reginald Owen. "Maurice Ravel." *ML* 2 (1921), pp. 274-283.
13. Ravel, Maurice. "What I Think of Modern Music." *Etude* 51 (1933), p. 571.
14. *Revue Musicale, La* 6 (April 1925); 19 (Dec 1938); 20 (Jan 1939), (Feb 1939), entire issues devoted to Ravel (in French).
15. Rosen, Charles. "Where Ravel ends and Debussy begins." *HiFi* 9 (May 1959), pp. 42-44.
16. Sabaneyev, Leonid L. "Maurice Ravel." *Mus Opinion* (Aug 1938).

Music

Study (Miniature) Scores

1. String Quartet in F major: *IMC*.

Playing Parts and Scores

2. String Quartet in F major: New York: International Music Company, 1951.
3. *Trio pour piano, violon et violoncelle.* Paris: Durand, 1915; Philadelphia: Elkan-Vogel, 1915; New York: International Music Company, 1944.
4. *Introduction et Allegro* for Harp solo, Flute, Clarinet, String Quartet. Paris: Durand, 1906.
5. *Sonate pour violon et piano.* Paris: Durand, 1927; Philadelphia: Elkan-Vogel, 1927.
6. *Sonate pour violon et violoncelle.* Paris: Durand, 1968; Philadelphia: Elkan-Vogel, 1968.

OUTLINE XV

BÉLA BARTÓK (1881 - 1945)

I. Life

1881   Born in the small town of Nagyszentmiklós, Hungary (now Sannicolaul Mare, Romania) on March 25.

1889   His father died and Béla and his mother lived in what is now Czechoslovakia and Romania. Taught music by his mother.

1891   First public appearance as a composer and pianist in Pozsony, now Bratislava in Czechoslovakia.

1893   Studied with László Erkel. Wrote a number of compositions in a romantic vein, strongly influenced by Johannes Brahms and Ernö Dohnányi.

1899   Entered the Royal Academy of Music in Budapest and remained there until 1909. Studied piano with István Thoman and composition with Hans Koessler, a pupil of Brahms. Studied music by Richard Wagner and Franz Liszt, but sought new ways of composing.

1902   Impressed by the music of Richard Strauss, but soon joined the national movement in Hungary and began in 1905 a thorough study of eastern European folk music, especially Hungarian peasant music.

1907   Appointed Professor of Piano at the Royal Academy of Music in Budapest. Devoted himself to composition, research in the field of folk music, teaching and recital tours in Europe as a pianist.

1908   Composed his first important chamber work, *String Quartet, No. 1, Op. 7.*

1912   Lack of understanding of his music and other disappointments led him to withdraw from public life.

1917   Success of the ballet *The Wooden Prince* and the one-act opera *Bluebird's Castle.*

1920   Returned to a more active life with concerts in England and France.

1923   Married for the second time.

1927   First trip to the United States where he played his own compositions during the 1927-1828 concert season.

1934   Resigned from his position at the Academy of Music in order to devote his full time to composing and the publication of folk music with Zoltán Kodály. The two are said to have collected over 6000 songs.

1940   Returned to the United States to avoid the occupation of Hungary, but was plagued by financial difficulties and ill health.

1942   Awarded a Doctor of Music degree from Columbia University and commissioned to edit a collection of Jugoslav folk songs.

1943   Lectured at Harvard University until his health forced his retirement.

1945   Died of leukemia on September 26 at the West Side Hospital, New York.

II. Catalogue of Chamber Music

A. Early Chamber Works (unpublished)
1. Piano Quartet (1898)
2. String Quartet (1899)
3. Quintet (1899) (probably incomplete)
4. Piano Quintet (1904)

B. Published Chamber Works
1. Violin and Piano Sonata (1903)

2. String Quartet No. 1, Op. 7 (1908)
3. String Quartet No. 2, Op. 17 (1914-1917)
4. Sonata No. 1 for Violin and Piano (1921)
5. Sonata No. 2 for Violin and Piano (1922)
6. String Quartet No. 3 (1927)
7. String Quartet No. 4 (1928)
8. 44 Duos for Two Violins (1931)
9. String Quartet No. 5 (1934)
10. String Quartet No. 6 (1939)
11. Contrasts for Violin, Clarinet and Piano (1938)
12. Sonata for Solo Violin (1943-1944)

III. Chamber Music

A. The six string quartets represent the essence of Bartók's style and the progressive development of his own personal and highly individual creative idiom.
B. Influences
   1. His early, unpublished compositions were influenced by the music of Johannes Brahms and about 1902 by the music of Franz Liszt and the German romanticist Richard Strauss.
   2. His contact with eastern European folk music, particularly Hungarian peasant melodies in 1905, resulted in an interest which exerted a strong influence throughout his entire creative life.
      a. This influence is reflected in freedom from major and minor tonalities, modal, pentatonic and irregular scales, quick changes of tempo, strong off-beat accents and powerful "Bulgarian rhythms."
   3. In 1939 he stated that the composers from whom he had learned the most were Bach (counterpoint), Beethoven (form) and Debussy (release from conventional harmony). At another time he wrote that his "ideal was not so much the art of Bach or Mozart as that of Beethoven."
C. Structure
   1. Bartók developed a highly individualistic treatment of the classical sonata, rondo and A - B - A forms with many modifications, unusual features and alterations.
   2. Movements are integrated by the cyclic idea of using themes or motives from earlier movements which are interrelated and varied with many transformations. The "arch-form" (A - B - C - B - A), a one-movement form (A - B - A - B) and a recurring "motto" theme were important aspects of his formal structures.
D. Melody
   1. The themes were usually constructed of a number of short "germ-motives" which were used in ever changing forms, often providing material for a movement or even an entire quartet.
      a. There are, however, melodies in the style of Hungarian folksongs, and themes which are true melodies.
E. Counterpoint
   1. Free use of imitation, canon, retrograde, inversion and fugal techniques are common, mostly in linear (non-harmonic) counterpoint, particularly in the later quartets.
F. Harmony
   1. The harmonic texture increased in dissonance and harshness by 1) linear counterpoint, 2) the chromatic scale with all notes of equal importance, 3) replacing diatonic notes with chromatics, 4) non-functional chords, 5) bitonal harmonies and 6) chords with added major and minor seconds, and perfect and augmented fourths.
   2. The tonality is free and usually indefinite and complex, but centered around or "on" a certain note.

IV. Six String Quartets

A. Quartet No. 1, Op. 7 (1908) (Lento - Allegretto - Allegro vivace)
  1. Although the chromaticism of Wagner is still apparent in both harmony and melody, the First Quartet marks the beginning of Bartók's break with the tradition of the German romantics Wagner and Brahms. In the Allegro vivace the influence of Hungarian peasant songs is evident.
  2. Lento (A - B - A form)
     a. All the movements are linked by the thematic derivations of motives in the opening phrase in double canon (meas. 1-2), in the Allegretto (meas. 20-21) and in the Allegro (meas. 5). Thematic elements of measure 6 in the Lento are used throughout the quartet.
     b. The second section (meas. 33) contains an impressionistic passage (meas. 45) in parallel thirds resembling Debussy. A transition to the Allegretto is *attacca*.
  3. Allegretto (free sonata form)
     a. Exposition
        1) The first theme group is made up of three motives: 1) measures 4-7; 2) measures 18-21; and 3) measures 22-29, second violin.
        2) A transition to the second theme, similar to the melodic material of the first theme, introduces a new motive in the cello (meas. 43). This motive, reinforced by the first violin, accompanies the second theme (meas. 73).
        3) Second theme (meas. 73). Whole-tone impressionistic passages occur in measures 105, 112.
     b. The Development begins in measure 140 and the second theme reappears in measure 217.
     c. The Recapitulation (meas. 288) is a compressed and modified version of the Exposition. The whole-tone scale is an integral part of the conclusion of the movement (meas. 320-339, 356).
  4. Allegro vivace (sonata form)
     a. The Allegro vivace is preceded by an Allegro *Introduzione* with contrasting rhythmic (three upper strings) and improvisational cello solo sections including motives used in the Finale.
     b. Exposition
        1) The first theme group is made up of three motives: 1) measures 5-7, derived from the main theme of the Allegretto (meas. 20-21); 2) measures 8-11 in Hungarian folk rhythm; 3) measure 20.
        2) A new motive in syncopated rhythm is played by the first violin (meas. 66).
        3) A 12-measure Adagio episode (meas. 94) interrupts the return to the syncopated melody in measure 106.
     c. Development
        1) The first theme (meas. 134) is varied and leads to an imitative *grazioso* melody presented in fugato and accompanied by pizzicato chords in the cello (meas. 158).
     d. Recapitulation (meas. 250). The Coda makes use of repeated notes common to the beginning of the movement in the first violin (meas. 365) and are followed by a three-octave whole-tone scale on B-flat (meas. 374-376).
B. Quartet No. 2, Op. 17 (1915-1917) (Moderato - Allegro molto capriccioso - Lento) Dedicated to the Hungarian Waldbauer-Kerpely Quartet.
  1. The second quartet represents Bartók's first highly individulatistic and mature style with the complete integration of Hungarian folk music and the appearance (after the famous piano *Allegro Barbaro*, 1911) of the "barbaric" Bartók.
  2. Moderato (sonata form)
     a. Exposition
        1) The principal theme (meas. 2-7) is presented in the first violin.

SALEM COLLEGE SCHOOL OF MUSIC

2) A transition (meas. 8) is based on the first theme.

3) An expansive second theme group begins with a cantabile melody in the viola (meas. 27-28) and leads into the main second theme by first and second violins (meas. 32-45).

4) The closing theme (meas. 63-69) is supported by parallel fifths in the cello, reminiscent of Debussy.

b. The Development (meas. 69) transforms the first motive of the Exposition and uses it in imitation. A new motive is introduced in measure 82 and then inverted (meas. 83).

c. The Recapitulation (meas. 114) extends the expressive first subject. The second group is shortened.

d. The quiet 6/8 - 9/8 Coda (meas. 153-156) uses the A minor closing theme in the violins in octaves. It is accompanied by A major pizzicato chords on the cello in contrasting duple meter. The following two measures (157-158) continue the bitonality in D major-minor.

3. Allegro molto capriccioso (extended rondo form)

a. The Introduction (meas. 1-7) of the "barbaric" movement is largely composed of two tritones (B - F and E - B-flat filled in) and has strong rhythmic drive.

b. The first rondo theme group (meas. 12-24) is divided into three motives: 1) measure 12; 2) measure 16, and 3) measure 22. Note the minor third is an essential characteristic of this theme.

c. The first episode makes elaborate use of the filled-in tritone of the Introduction. A new theme (meas. 139-143) leads back to the recapitulation of the rondo (meas. 153) in more elaborate form.

d. The second episode (meas. 216) uses the introductory rocking tritone figure as its basis; several measure pauses give the feeling of a hesitant beginning. After a transitory reminder of the undulating minor thirds (meas. 284, 290, 294) of the main theme, a dolce motive (meas. 304) is developed in a slower section resembling a Trio.

e. The rondo reappears transformed into 3/4 (meas. 391) and reaches a high point (meas. 444) of great passion, *con gran passione*.

f. The Coda (meas. 479), beginning after a strong pizzicato chord, varies material from the rondo section with polyrhythms. The movement closes with a fortissimo statement of the minor third of the main theme.

4. Lento

a. The last movement is a combination of Hungarian and impressionistic elements. It is made up of four short sections, seemingly unrelated except for a unifying cadential figure (meas. 19-21; 25-27; 29-31; 65-67; 69-70) which brings the quartet to a close.

C. Quartet No. 3 (1927) (Prima parte - Secunda parte - Ricapitulazione della prima parte - Coda) Dedicated to the Musical Fund Society of Philadelphia.

1. This quartet, the one of the six least accessible and most difficult to understand, shows Bartók at the pinnacle of his intellectual modernism. It follows a period of experimentation and development toward an objective "expressionistic" style of uncompromising harshness.

2. The quartet is in two movements (Prima parte, Secunda parte) which are to be played without break. The Second Part is followed by an abbreviated and varied *Ricapitulazione* of the First Part and, in turn, is followed by a Coda thematically based on the Second Part.

3. The First Part (Moderato) is divided into three section (A - B - A).

a. Section A (meas. 1-46).

    1)   The first melodic phrase (meas. 2-5) is in three parts and, with two four-note motives (meas. 6-7), includes most of the motives used in the First Part.

        a)   Characteristic repetitions of a single note and long pedal points occur throughout.

    2)   A new section, Più andante (meas. 35-42), uses a bitonal ostinato (in lower strings) derived from the main theme (meas. 6-7).

  b.   Section B (meas. 47-83)

    1)   A new four-note motive is followed by brutal double and triple stops for all strings (meas. 54).

    2)   The following passage, Più lento (meas. 64), makes use of twelve-tone chromaticism in a modified form of the main theme.

  c.   Section A (meas. 83-112)

    1)   The first theme appears as a folk-like melody in octaves in the middle strings.

4.   The Second Part (Allegro) is divided into two contrasting subjects: 1) a rhythmic dance-like tune of open parallel triads played by the cello (meas. 5-11) and 2) a kind of variant of the first theme (meas. 26-29) presented in sixteenth notes by the first violin, accompanied by the first subject. There are frequent changes of meter (2/4, 3/4, 5/8, 6/8, 3/8).

  a.   A third theme, related to the first, enters in the viola and cello at measure 80. Based on the whole-tone scale, it makes use of syncopation and the descending fourth.

  b.   After the development of the second theme (meas. 182), a varied form of the theme becomes the basis of a fugato section (meas. 242). The main theme returns (meas. 284) in the cello in canonic imitation with the first violin (meas. 285).

  c.   Glissandos of melodic fragments (meas. 353-360), rough percussive chords (meas. 377-383) and *molto vibrato* in all four strings (meas. 397-399) lead to the Recapitulation of the first movement.

5.   The Recapitulation of the First Part (Moderato) has the material of the first part abbreviated and altered extensively.

6.   The Coda (Allegro molto) is an abbreviated recapitulation of the Second Part. The first theme of the Second Part appears in stretto (meas. 3-5) and the second theme also enters in stretto (meas. 23-26) and later is accompanied with extensive descending glissandos (meas. 77-83).

  a.   The third theme, a variant of the first, enters briefly in double stops in the cello (meas. 83) and again inverted (meas. 94) in double stops in the first violin. After rapid tremolandos (meas. 110) and a glissando in all instruments (meas. 116), a series of harsh, brutal chords concludes the quartet.

D.   Quartet No. 4 (1928) (Allegro - Prestissimo, con sordino - Non troppo lento - Allegretto pizzicato - Allegro molto) Dedicated to the Pro Arte Quartet.

1.   This quartet in five movements, generally considered Bartók's greatest achievement, is a concentrated work with emphasis on linear counterpoint, a harsh harmonic idiom with close intervals, feverish rhythmic drive and special sound effects. The themes are often formed by the development of short motives.

2.   Here Bartók reaches the ultimate in his powers of construction which are realized in each movement and the "arch-form" of the five movements.

  a.   In the arch-form the first and fifth, second and fourth movements share materials; the third is an independent movement which forms the cornerstone as follows: I - II - III - II - I. A symmetrical relationship also exists in the tonalities. The first and last movements are on C, the second a third above on E, the fourth a third below on A-flat.

3.   Allegro (sonata form)

  a.   Exposition

    1)   Principal theme group (meas. 1-7). The germ-motive in the cello (meas. 7) becomes important in this movement and throughout the quartet. The subsidiary

theme in the cello (meas. 14) begins a transition of imitative passages leading to full chords (meas. 37) and the closing section (meas. 44).

 b. Development

  1) The first subject enters (meas. 49) and is followed by a short trill-like figure which continues during the Development. The second subject in the cello (meas. 60) is imitated in inversion by the viola. The germ-motive (meas. 7) appears inverted in the cello and viola (meas. 84), straight (meas. 85) and leads to the Recapitulation (meas. 92).

 c. Recapitulation

  1) The order of themes in the Recapitulation is reversed; the germ-motive appears first (meas. 92) and the main theme then in stretto (meas. 104).

 d. The Coda, made up principally of elaborate use of the germ-motive, closes with a powerful statement of the germ-motive.

4. Prestissimo, con sordino (sectional form)

 a. The first theme is a rising and falling chromatic line (meas. 106) presented in the cello and viola an octave apart.

 b. The middle section (meas. 32) includes the return of the first theme in imitation (meas. 54).

 c. The Trio section (meas. 75) is characterized by a motive built on diminished thirds and an ostinato-like accompaniment of undulating minor seconds in the viola. When the accompaniment figure ultimately takes over all parts (meas. 102) it is introduced by a quintole figure which becomes a prominent figure in a new section (meas. 145-150). A unique effect is produced by glissandos in all parts (meas. 137).

 d. A new section (meas. 145) uses the quintole figure in scale-like passages broken by pizzicato chords.

 e. The return of the chromatic first theme takes place in measure 189. Pizzicato glissando fifth chords in the cello and arco glissandos and trills (meas. 213) bring the movement to a close.

5. Non troppo lento (A - B - A)

 a. This central movement in the "arch-form" is more homophonic than the two previous movements.

 b. The main theme is a recitative-like melody of Hungarian flavor in the cello (meas. 6) made up of embellishments, syncopation and drooping intervals. It is divided into three melodic units (meas. 6-13; meas. 14-21; meas. 22-34) and accompanied by chords played alternately non-vibrato and vibrato.

 c. In the B section (meas. 34-54) the first violin creates an improvisatory effect characteristic of the impressionistic style.

 d. An Agitato section (meas. 42) anticipates the return of the first idea in the cello (meas. 55) and mirrored in the first violin (meas. 56).

 e. A Coda (meas. 64) uses material from the improvisatory section.

6. Allegretto pizzicato

 a. All kinds of pizzicato are included in this movement: single notes (meas. 1); double stops (meas. 13); broken chords (meas. 45); unbroken chords (meas. 1); guitar-like rapid repetition (meas. 78) and the hard snap on the fingerboard (meas. 90).

 b. The first theme (meas. 6 in the viola) is diatonic, rather than chromatic as it appeared in the second movement.

 c. The second part (meas. 45) is related to the Trio theme in the second movement (meas. 75).

 d. The first theme, changed essentially into a whole-tone melody, reappears (meas. 78) and is followed by imitative passages and stretto (meas. 106-111) to the end.

7. Allegro molto

 a. The fifth movement is thematically related to the first and is introduced by eleven measures of broad, multivoiced chords.

    b.   The first theme (meas. 14), accompanied by asymmetrically accented chords, is developed from a motive related to the subsidiary theme in the first movement (meas. 14). This motive and its inversion are used throughout most of this section. It takes on a scherzando character in measure 102. A repetition of the opening multivoiced chords (meas. 121) introduces the Trio section (meas. 151).

    c.   Trio section (meas. 151)

        1)   A new motive occurs in the first violin and viola (meas. 156) accompanied by the open strings of the second violin and cello.

        2)   The germ-motive of the first theme appears in the cello (meas. 162) and is developed throughout the remainder of the movement.

E.   Quartet No. 5 (1934) (Allegro - Adagio molto - Scherzo - Andante - Finale: Allegro vivace) Dedicated to Mrs. Elizabeth Sprague Coolidge.

  1.   The Fifth Quartet resembles the Fourth in the use of the "arch-form" and symmetrical patterns. The second and fourth movements are slow, however, and reveal a more relaxed lyrical character. The central movement is a Scherzo which makes use of Bulgarian rhythmic patterns of 9/8 and 10/8 meter subdivided in various ways. The Recapitulation of the first movement reverses the themes and also the thematic materials.

  2.   Allegro (sonata form)

    a.   Exposition

        1)   The first thematic group is divided into three motives: 1) measure 1; 2) the second half of measure 4 and measure 5 (viola and cello); 3) the quintole motive at the end of measure 8 and measure 9 (viola and cello). The first section closes in measure 13.

        2)   The second section (meas. 14-25) is made up of material not used again.

        3)   The transitional theme (meas. 25) has irregular cross rhythms indicated by dotted barlines. The meters form a rhythmic canon.

        4.   The second subject (meas. 44), lyrical in nature, is presented in imitation and the Exposition comes to a close in measure 58.

    b.   The Development (meas. 59) has the first and second motives combined. The quasi-Bulgarian rhythmic motive from measure 25 is combined with a variation of the quintole motive (meas. 87). A new form of the quintole motive is combined with the first repeated note motive (meas. 112).

    c.   The Recapitulation (meas. 126), in general, presents the Exposition in mirror. The themes are reversed in order and are inverted also.

        1)   The second subject (meas. 44) is inverted (meas. 132) and appears before the first subject group in inversion (meas. 167).

    d.   The Coda (meas. 177) makes use of fragments of the first and second subjects.

  3.   Adagio molto (ternary form: A - B - A)

    a.   There are no real themes but only motives or fragments combined to form a sectional structure.

    b.   After an introduction of trills and motives, section A (meas. 10) has characteristic motives presented in the first violin with a chorale in sustained chords in the lower strings.

    c.   Section B is based on a lyrical theme of Hungarian folk-like quality (meas. 31).

    d.   Section A, modified, returns with the chorale (meas. 46), and elements of the Introduction make up the Coda (meas. 50).

  4.   Scherzo: Alla bulgarese (vivace) - Trio

    a.   The Bulgarian rhythms of the Scherzo are divided into an asymmetrical pattern of 4 + 2 + 3 eighth notes.

    b.   The Scherzo is divided into three sections, the first (meas. 1-30) being made up principally of an arpeggio figure. The second section (meas. 30-50) has a theme of folk dance character, and the arpeggio figure returns (meas. 50) to complete the Scherzo.

        1)   The Bulgarian rhythms of the Trio are more complex. Simultaneous with the

rhythm of 3 + 2 + 2 + 3 eighths generally in the first violin may appear rhythms of 2 + 3 + 3 + 2 or 2 + 3 + 2 + 3 eighths. The first violin develops an ostinato which recurs 60 times in various transpositions.

   2)   The da capo Scherzo is a varied and extended restatement of the first Scherzo.

5.   Andante (ternary form: A - B - A)

   a.   Like the second movement, the sectional structure of the Andante does not admit of a theme but only motives.

   b.   The introductory section uses pizzicato, pizzicato glissandi and trills. The middle section (meas. 43) expressively ornaments the lyrical theme of the second movement. The return of section A (meas. 82) is barely recognized, nevertheless the repeated chords (meas. 95) confirm it. The ascending triple stop glissando chords in the cello bring the movement to a mysterious close.

6.   Finale: Allegro vivace (sonata form)

   a.   The Finale is a contrapuntal tour de force full of imitative devices: canon, inversion, stretto, retrograde, fugue.

   b.   The Introduction (meas. 1-14) is made up of a four-note motive played in unison and octaves.

   c.   In the Exposition the main theme (meas. 14-18) is a free inversion of the main theme of the first movement. The texture is frequently two-voice (meas. 35-36) and four-voice (meas. 43-44) imitation with scale-wise material. Transition (meas. 183). A new theme, marked Più presto, *scorrevole* (flowing) (meas. 202) is presented in imitation and inversion, at times fragmented. A transition (meas. 350), using material from the introduction, leads into the Development.

   d.   The Development (meas. 368-479) is a fugue with the subject (meas. 370), first in the viola marked *oscuro*, being derived from the main theme of the first movement. A harmonic background is supplied by a drone-like ostinato in the cello and a percussive note pattern repeated in the violins.

   e.   Recapitulation (meas. 480)

     1)   An unusual transitional passage in A major (meas. 700-720), marked Allegretto, *con indifferenza*, and to be played *meccanico*, makes use of an ordinary melody with simple harmony. In measures 711-720 the melody is repeated in B-flat major against harmonies in A major.

   f.   The Coda (meas. 721), to be played *con slancio* (with dash), is in stretto and ends on a unison B-flat.

F.   Quartet No. 6 (1939) (Vivace - Marcia - Burletta - Mesto) Dedicated to the Kolisch Quartet.

  1.   Bartók returns to a more "classical" style in this quartet: greater simplicity, less harsh harmonies, more transparent texture, clarity of form. The "arch-form" was discarded and a "motto" theme employed as a unifying device. The "motto" was used to introduce each of the three movements and became the integral material for the Finale.

  2.   Mesto - Vivace - Più mosso, pesante (sonata form)

   a.   The movement begins with the "mesto" motto presented by the solo viola (meas. 1-13) followed immediately by a pesante section (meas. 14-23) in which the four strings present the motto in augmentation (meas. 18-23).

   b.   The Exposition is made up of two themes. The first thematic complex appears in the Vivace (meas. 24-80). The second theme (meas. 81) is made up of two measures of a quarter, two eighths and a quartet note followed by the reverse, an eighth, two quarters and an eighth. In the closing section (meas. 99, Vivacissimo, agitato) reference is made to the first theme (meas. 109, 117) and second theme (meas. 111).

   c.   The Development (meas. 158), beginning with the main theme in augmentation (meas. 158-165, pesante), uses the main theme in the viola and cello (meas. 166-168) accompanied by the last four notes of the theme in inverse retrograde in the violins. A variant of the first theme may be seen in the ostinato in the first violin and cello (meas. 180-193). Expansion of the theme may be noted in measures 197 (cello) to 256.

    d.   The Recapitulation (meas. 287) states the themes in classical order and closes with some suggestion of the first theme.

3.   Marcia

    a.   The introductory "mesto" theme is presented in the cello with a single contrapuntal part duplicated in three octaves by the upper strings. A concluding four-note motive in the second violin anticipates the Marcia.

    b.   The Marcia (meas. 1-79), in small ternary form, is followed by a rhapsodic Trio (meas. 80-122) with the melody high in the cello. Tremolos and four-voice chords strummed by the viola lead to a quasi cadenza (meas. 115) in all four instruments. The return of the Marcia is marked by doubling of parts, some inversion and canonic imitation in harmonics.

4.   Mesto - Burletta: Moderato - Andantino

    a.   The "mesto" introduction is a three-part setting with the viola entering in measure 10 to reinforce the first violin an octave lower.

    b.   The Burletta, a "barbaric" movement, uses discords, percussive chords, pizzicato and glissandi. Quarter tones are played against true tones to create an out-of-tune effect. "Au talon" is frequently prescribed.

    c.   The Trio, a lyrical middle section, has two themes freely derived from the two themes of the first movement: theme I (meas. 70) from measure 24 of the first movement and theme II (meas. 78) from measure 81, movement I.

    d.   The Recapitulation (meas. 97), in contrast to the first section, is slightly modified and is played pizzicato. A new triplet motive is added (meas. 115).

    e.   In the Coda (meas. 123-153) the progress of the burlesque is interrupted three times (meas. 135, 138, 142) with the second theme of the Trio.

5.   Mesto

    a.   The introductory "motto" theme of the first movement supplies the principal material for the last movement. The two subjects, also from the first movement, are restated: the first, molto tranquillo (meas. 46), and the second, più dolce, lontano (meas. 55). Amidst the ominous unrest suggested by tremolo chords (meas. 75-76) and sudden outbursts of crescendoing chords (meas. 78-81), the "motto" theme reappears transfigured (meas. 81) and brings to a fitting conclusion this great series of string quartets.

V. Two Sonatas for Violin and Piano (1921, 1922)

    A.   The Two Sonatas for Violin and Piano were written for Miss Jelly d'Arányi at the close of Bartók's so-called experimental or "expressionist" period. The sonatas are full of original and contrasting musical ideas which are developed in a unique way. The harmonic idiom in the piano part is often harsh with percussive sound-masses and clashes of close intervals, but there are moments of lyricism.

    1.   During this period Bartók approached the principle of the twelve-tone series of the Schönberg school from time to time, but never accepted it completely. With the completion of the sonatas for violin and piano he turned to a more contrapuntal style of writing.

    B.   Sonata No. 1 for Violin and Piano (1921)

    1.   Allegro appassionato

    a.   A rhapsodic movement in free sonata form with many changes of tempo and time signatures.

    b.   The second theme (meas. 16) is characteristic of the Schönberg school with its wide skips and avoidance of repeating the same note. The turbulent middle section leads to a recapitulation (p. 14, no. 20) and the movement closes quietly.

    2.   Adagio
       a.   Ternary form without a regular recapitulation. The movement opens with a lyrical recitative for violin followed by a short section accompanied with parallel moving chords. Another recitative with changing meters (p. 21, no. 2) is followed by another section with parallel moving chords. There are some suggestions of the twelve-tone technique in melodic lines.
       b.   The middle section (p. 22, no. 4) introduces an elaborate accompaniment and passages for double stops. The brief final section is introduced by a short recitative for violin (p. 24, no. 10) and followed by parallel moving harmonies.
    3.   Allegro
       a.   The form is a very free rondo in the style of a lively peasant dance. Bitonality between the violin and piano accompaniment is characteristic of the movement. Strong accent and off-beat rhythm add increasing vitality.
       b.   The main theme, separated by new material, recurs considerably varied in the piano (p. 34, no. 12) and in the violin (p. 42, no. 33; p. 48, no. 44). The movement closes with a mixolydian scale on B and a final E major chord over a piano C-sharp major-minor chord.
  C.   Sonata No. 2 for Violin and Piano (1922)
    1.   The second sonata has only two movements which are played without a break. The work is concentrated and approaches the limits of so-called atonality, although Bartók considered it to be "very freely" in the key of C.
    2.   Molto moderato
       a.   The first movement is in a free three-part form, bordering on sonata form and somewhat improvisatory in character.
       b.   A quiet four-measure "introduction," consisting of two widely separated notes, introduces in the violin an expressive lyrical theme of close intervals which more or less dominate the relatively short first movement. A second thematic idea with wide intervals appears (p. 4, no. 2) and the two ideas are developed in a highly original manner.
       c.   There are frequent changes in time signatures and tempos (pp. 3, 4, 6), cluster chords in the piano with glissandi in the violin (p. 4, meas. 2, 3), glissando harmonics with mute (p. 4, meas. 7-14), tone masses of close intervals and purely instrumental effects (p. 9, meas. 4-5).
       d.   The middle section concludes with a brief recapitulation or coda in the mood of the beginning.
    3.   Allegretto
       a.   The second movement (p. 11) is a dance-like finale to the second sonata and has some of the characteristics of a three-part or free rondo form.
       b.   The main theme is announced pizzicato by the violin following a few quiet chords on the piano which establish the rhythm. The theme is based on scale lines with strong cross accents and forms a unifying device throughout the movement.
       c.   Repeated notes and chords (p. 12) form a contrasting idea with the main theme throughout the middle section. There are whole-tone clusters with violin glissandi (pp. 20, 21) and scherzando sections (p. 24, no. 3; p. 30).
       d.   The closing section (p. 31, no. 43) returns to the scale-line theme and closes pianissimo with open fifths in the piano and harmonics in the violin.

VI.   44 Duos for Two Violins (1931)

  A.   The Duos, with two exceptions, are all based on peasant melodies. Like the 85 piano pieces "For Children" (1908-1909, revised in 1944) and the "Mikrokosmos" (1926-1939), which includes 153 progressive pieces for piano, the Duos have a pedagogical aim. They are of great artistic value and a key to the idiom of Bartók and a preparation for more difficult works.

B.   The Duos are all very short, not over a minute and a half in length, but they include many of Bartók's rhythmic and contrapuntal devices. Above all, they reveal the remarkable way in which he used and reconstructed folk music.

1.   The "Harvest Song" (No. 33) is an example of bitonal writing, irregular meters, canon (meas. 6-15), changes of tempo, stretto (Tempo II, meas. 21), and above all his remarkable use of folk material.

VII.   Contrasts for Violin, Clarinet and Pianoforte (1938)

A.   Consist of three contrasting pieces commissioned by Benny Goodman and Joseph Szigeti. The work was intended for virtuoso players with Bartók at the piano. Cadenzas are provided for the violin and clarinet. Two clarinets (in A and B-flat) are used in the first two pieces and two violins (one with *scordatura* tuning) are required in the last piece.

B.   Recruiting Dance (*Verbunkos*)

1.   A stately, stylized Hungarian dance with many alternating sections in varied tempos and styles, but usually dissonant and strongly rhythmic. Glissandos are employed in the piano part (meas. 45-54). The theme on the A clarinet at the beginning of the movement, accompanied by pizzicato chords, resembles somewhat the *Marcia* in the sixth string quartet (1939). The piece closes with a cadenza (two variants are included) for the clarinet in A.

C.   Relaxation (*Pihenő*)

1.   This quiet, melodic Lento, interrupted with brief forte interludes, was added to a planned two-movement rhapsody and the title changed to "Contrasts." The clarinet in A is again called for. There are numerous changes in meter, particularly at the beginning of the piece (4/4, 3/2, 5/4, 4/4, 3/4, etc.).

D.   Fast Dance (*Sebes*)

1.   A strongly rhythmic piece (Allegro vivace) resembling in general character the finale from the first sonata for violin and piano (1931). The powerful rhythms are emphasized in the piano by highly dissonant chords and tone clusters (meas. 103-111; 165-168). There are many changes in tempo, sudden changes in volume, cross accents and irregular meters (meas. 81-88).

a.   The violin *scordatura* tuning begins the piece (meas. 1-30). The E string is lowered to E-flat and the G string is raised to G-sharp. The violin with the usual tuning is taken at measure 30.

2.   The middle section (Più mosso, meas. 132-168) is in the "Bulgarian rhythm." The basic unit is 13/8 divided into two measures as follows: ♩. ♩ ♩. | ♩ ♩. or ♩. ♩ | ♩. ♩ | ♩. . In this section the clarinet in B-flat is changed to the clarinet in A and returns to the B-flat clarinet at Tempo I (meas. 169).

3.   The Recapitulation (meas. 169) includes a cadenza for violin. The Coda (meas. 287) introduces in all instruments a series of repeated high notes with grace notes which produces an effect bordering on the comic. The work closes with a return to the original tempo (meas. 313).

VIII.   Sonata for Solo Violin (1944)

A.   Bartók's next to the last complete work was written in the United States for Yehudi Menuhin who also edited the work for publication. Quarter-tones were called for in the original manuscript but the score was printed without them. Bartók's interest in the music of pre-classical composers, especially Bach, began in the early 1920's and undoubtedly inspired this modern example of a masterly developed uncompromising work for solo violin.

1. The Sonata is in four movements. The first two are highly concentrated and make use of many contrapuntal devices in his own musical language. The last two are a relaxed slow movement and a lively Presto. There are no key signatures, and the complete work concludes with a G major chord.

B. Tempo di Ciacona
 1. Not a movement in pre-classical chaconne form (variations on a ground bass), but in three sections somewhat similar to sonata form.
 2. Two strong chords introduce the first section, middle section (meas. 53) and final section (meas. 91).

C. Fuga
 1. Begins Risoluto, non troppo vivo with a four-part exposition of the subject with the tonal answer a fifth above (meas. 5). The subject enters again at the octave above (meas. 10) accompanied by the countersubject and a third voice. The answer enters, somewhat modified, an octave above (meas. 15). Episodes follow with many contrapuntal devices using material derived from the exposition and references to the subject (meas. 37, 44). There is use of pizzicato (meas. 65-72) and plucking the string so that it rebounds against the fingerboard (snap pizzicato) (meas. 69).
 2. The Fuga concludes with a chord marked *f* which diminishes with a glissando to *ppp*. After a pause of three beats the first two notes of the subject (C, E-flat) are heard *ff*.

D. Melodia
 1. Following the remarkable technical and musical creation of the Ciacona and Fuga, the Melodia provides a quiet interlude before the finale.
 2. The simple appealing melody, marked Adagio, is followed by a contrasting middle section, Un poco più andante, with chordal writing and the use of the mute. After a cadenza-like passage, the music returns to the original tempo and general melodic style with a brief passage for violin harmonics. The movement concludes pianissimo with five four-note chords without mute.
 3. Each phrase in the first and last sections concludes with a short figure using harmonics.

E. Presto
 1. Three main sections consisting of rapid passages in sixteenth notes separated by two contrasting episodes with more use of double stops.
 2. The mute is used in the first two main sections. A special effect is the taking off and putting on the mute while the left hand plucks an open string (meas. 196, 262).

SELECTED BIBLIOGRAPHY

Books

1. Bartók, Béla. *Béla Bartók Letters*, ed. János Demény; tr. Péter Balabán and István Farkas. New York: St. Martin's Press, 1971; London: Faber & Faber, 1971.
2. *Bartók Studies*, ed. Todd Crow. Detroit: Information Coordinators, 1976.
3. *Béla Bartók, A Memorial Review*. New York: Boosey & Hawkes, 1950.
4. Deri, Otto. *Exploring Twentieth Century Music*. New York: Holt, Rinehart and Winston, 1968. (Bartók: pp. 222-262)
5. Dommett, Kenneth. *Bartók*. London: Novello, 1978.
6. Fassett, Agatha. *The Naked Face of Genius; Béla Bartók's American Years*. Boston: Houghton Mifflin, 1958.
7. Haraszti, Emil. *Béla Bartók; His Life and Works*, tr. Dorothy Swainson. Paris: The Lyrebird Press, 1938.
8. Helm, Everett. "Bartók," in *European Music in the Twentieth Century*, ed. Howard Hartog. Westport, CT: Greenwood Press, 1977.
9. ——————*Bartók*. London: Faber & Faber, 1972.

10. Kárpáti, János. *Bartók's String Quartets*, tr. Fred Macnicol. London: Corvina Press, 1975.
11. Kroó, György. *A Guide to Bartók*, tr. Ruth Pataki and Mariá Steiner. London: Corvina Press, 1974.
12. Lendvai, Ernö. *Béla Bartók; An Analysis of His Music*. London: Kahn & Averill, 1971.
13. Lesznai, Lajos. *Bartók*, tr. Percy M. Young. London: J. M. Dent, 1973.
14. Moreux, Serge. *Bartók*, tr. G. S. Fraser and Erik de Mauny. London: Harvell Press, 1953.
15. Perle, George. *The String Quartets of Béla Bartók*. New York: Dover Publications, 1967.
16. Seiber, Mátyás. *The String Quartets of Béla Bartók*. London: Boosey & Hawkes, 1945.
17. Stevens, Halsey. *The Life and Music of Béla Bartók*, 2nd edition. New York: Oxford University Press, 1964; paperback, 1969. (Chamber Music: pp. 170-226)
18. Szigeti, Joseph. *With Strings Attached*. London: Cassell, 1949.
19. Thompson, Kenneth. *A Dictionary of Twentieth Century Composers, 1911-1971*. New York: St. Martin's Press, 1973. (Bartók: pp. 17-41)
20. Whittall, Arnold. *Music Since the First World War*. London: J. M. Dent, 1977. (Bartók: pp. 31-50)

Articles

1. Abraham, Gerald. "The Bartók of the Quartets." *ML* 26 (1945), pp. 185-194.
2. ———————"Bartók: String Quartet, No. 6." *MR* 3 (1942), pp. 72-73.
3. Babbitt, Milton. "The String Quartets of Béla Bartók." *MQ* 35 (1949), pp. 377-385.
4. Balogh, Ernö. "Personal Glimpses of Béla Bartók." *Pro Musica* 7 (1928).
5. Becker, Harry C. "Béla Bartók and his Credo." *MA* 47 (Dec 17, 1927).
6. Bowie, Michael. "Tempo Indications in Bartók's String Quartet No. 1." *Strad* 89 (1978), p. 397.
7. Browne, Arthur G. "Béla Bartók." *ML* 12 (1931), pp. 35-45.
8. Calvocoressi, M. D. "Béla Bartók, an Introduction." *Monthly Musical Record* 52 (1922).
9. Carner, Mosco. "Béla Bartók." *Listener* (Nov 1945).
10. Chapman, Ernest. "Béla Bartók; an Estimate and Appreciation." *Tempo* 9 (Dec 1945).
11. Chittum, Donald. "The Synthesis of Materials and Devices in Non-Serial Counterpoint." *MR* 31 (1970), pp. 123-135.
12. Cowell, Henry. "Bartók and His Violin Concerto." *Tempo* 8 (Sept 1944), pp. 4-6.
13. Crankshaw, Geoffrey. "Bartók's Quartet II." *Mus & Musicians* 16 (Jan 1968), p. 58.
14. Cross, Anthony. "Debussy and Bartók." *MT* 108 (1967), pp. 125-127.
15. Dickinson, Alan E. "Back to the Bartók Quartets." *Mus Opinion* 99 (Nov 1975), p. 79.
16. Elston, Arnold. "Some Rhythmic Practices in Contemporary Music." *MQ* 42 (1956), pp. 319-322.
17. Forte, Allen. "Bartók's 'Serial' Composition." *MQ* 46 (1960), pp. 233-245.
18. Foss, Hubert J. "An Approach to Bartók." *Mus Opinion* 67 (Apr 1944).
19. Gilman, Lawrence. "Bartók Comes Back." *NYHT*, Oct 24, 1937.
20. Gombosi, Otto. "Béla Bartók, 1881-1945." *MQ* 32 (1946), pp. 1-11.
21. Gow, David. "Tonality and Structure in Bartók's First Two String Quartets." *MR* 34 (1973), pp. 259-271.
22. Howat, Roy. "Debussy, Ravel and Bartók; Towards Some New Concepts of Form." *ML* 58 (1977), pp. 285-293.
23. Jemnitz, Alexander. "Béla Bartók," tr. Theodore Baker. *MQ* 19 (1933), pp. 260-266.
24. Lang, Paul Henry. "Editorial." *MQ* 32 (1946), pp. 131-136.
25. Leichtentritt, Hugo. "On the Art of Béla Bartók." *MM* 6 (Mar-Apr 1929), pp. 3-11.
26. Long, N. G. "The Quartets of Béla Bartók." *Listener* (Mar 21, 1946).
27. Mason, Colin. "An Essay in Analysis: Tonality, Symmetry and Latent Serialism in Bartók's Fourth Quartet." *MR* 18 (1957), pp. 189-201.
28. ———————"Review of Bartók's Six Quartets." *Free Europe* (Nov 30, 1945).
29. Manesce, Jacques de. "Berg and Bartók." *MM* 21 (Jan-Feb 1944), pp. 76-81.

30. Menasce, Jacques de. "The Classicism of Béla Bartók." *MM* 23 (Spring 1946), pp. 83-88.
31. Monelle, Raymond. "Notes on Bartók's Fourth Quartet." *MR* 29 (1968), pp. 123-129.
32. –––––––"Bartók's Imagination in the Later Quartets." *MR* 31 (1970), pp. 70-81.
33. Moore, Douglas. "Homage to Bartók." *MM* 23 (Winter 1946), pp. 13-14.
34. Morgan, Robert P. "Bartók's Extraordinary Quartets." *HiFi* 20 (Sept 1970), pp. 58-61.
35. Nordwall, Ove. "Béla Bartók and Modern Music." *Studia Mus* 9, Nos. 3-4 (1967), pp. 265-280.
36. –––––––"The Original Version of Bartók's Sonata for Solo Violin." *Tempo* 74 (Autumn 1965), pp. 2-4.
37. Persichetti, Vincent. "Current Chronicle." *MQ* 35 (1949), pp. 122-126.
38. Rands, Bernard. "The Use of Canon in Bartók's Quartets." *MR* 18 (1957), pp. 183-188.
39. Richards, Denby. "Bartók Quartets, I." *Mus & Musicians* 16 (Jan 1968), p. 49.
40. Saminsky, Lazare. "Schönberg and Bartók, Pathbreakers." *MM* 1 (Feb 1924), pp. 27-28.
41. Seiber, Matyas. "Béla Bartók." *Monthly Musical Record* 75 (Nov 1945).
42. Sessions, Roger. "Béla Bartók." *Listener* (Jan 1946).
43. Suchoff, Benjamin. "Bartók's Second String Quartet; Stylistic Landmark." *Am Mus Tcr* 15, No. 2 (1965), pp. 30-32.
44. –––––––"Structure and Concept in Bartók's Sixth Quartet." *Tempo* 83 (Winter 1967-1968), pp. 2-11.
45. Travis, Roy. "Tonal Coherence in the First Movement of Bartók's Fourth String Quartet." *Music Forum* 2 (1970), pp. 298-371.
46. Trützschler, Heinz. "The Chamber Music of Bartók." *Mus J* 25 (May 1966), p. 25.
47. Vinton, John. "Bartók on His Own Music." *JAMS* 19 (1966), pp. 232-243.
48. –––––––"New Light on Bartók's Sixth Quartet." *MR* 25 (1964), pp. 224-238.
49. Weissmann, John S. "Bartók: An Estimate." *MR* 7 (1946), pp. 221-241.
50. –––––––"Bartók Festival in Budapest." *MR* 10 (1949), pp. 36-37.
51. Whitaker, Frank. "A Visit to Béla Bartók." *MT* 67 (1926).
52. Whittall, Arnold. "Bartók's Second String Quartet." *MR* 32 (1971), pp. 265-270.
53. Winrow, Barbara. "Allegretto con Indifferenza: A Study of the 'Barrel Organ' Episode in Bartók's Fifth Quartet." *MR* 32 (1971), pp. 102-106.
54. Yates, Peter. "Béla Bartók." *Partisan Review* 16 (1949), pp. 643-648.

Music

Study (Miniature) Scores

1. *String Quartets*, Nos. 1-6. New York: Boosey & Hawkes, 1939-1941.

Playing Parts and Scores

2. *Streichquartett*, Nos. 1, 6. New York: Boosey & Hawkes, 1941; Nos. 2, 3, 4, 5. Vienna: Universal-Edition.
3. *Quintetto per 2 violini, viola, violoncello e pianoforte* (1904). Budapest: Editio Musica, 1970.
4. *Deux Sonates pour Violon et Piano*. Vienna: Universal-Edition, 1923; New York: Boosey & Hawkes, 1950.
   a. *Première Sonate* (*UE* 7247)
   b. *Deuxième Sonate* (*UE* 7259)
5. *Sonate für Violine und Klavier* (1903). Budapest: Editio Musica, 1968.
6. *44 Duos* (1931). Vienna: Universal-Edition (*UE* 10452 a/b).
7. *Contrasts* for Violin, Clarinet and Piano (1938). New York: Boosey & Hawkes.

ABBREVIATIONS

Acta Mus — Acta Musicologica
Am Mus Tcr — American Music Teacher
BH — Boosey & Hawkes
c. — circa (about)
CE — Complete Works; Complete Edition
Current Mus — Current Musicology
DV — Dover Publications (Schubert)
ed. — edition, edited, editor
EE — E. Eulenberg Miniature Scores
Etude — Etude Music Magazine
HiFi/MA — HiFi/Musical America
IMC — International Music Company
JAMS — Journal of the American Musicological Society
K. — Köchel (Mozart)
KSS — Kalmus Study Score
Lea — Lea Pocket Score
M — music
MA — Musical America

MC — Musical Courier
meas. — measure
ML — Music and Letters
MM — Modern Music
MNW — Mozart Neue Ausgabe sämtlicher Werke
MQ — The Musical Quarterly
MT — Musical Times
Mus & Musicians — Music and Musicians
Mus Opinion — Musical Opinion
New Mus Rev — New Music Review
No. — number
NYHT — New York Herald Tribune
Op. — Opus
p. — page (pp. — pages)
PNM — Perspectives of New Music
tr. -— translation, translated, translator
v. — volume
Wg. — Werkgruppe (volume) (Mozart)

GENERAL BIBLIOGRAPHY

Books

1. Altmann, Wilhelm. *Kammermusik-Katalog*, 6th ed. Leipzig: Hofmeister, 1945.
2. Cobbett, Walter William. *Cyclopedic Survey of Chamber Music*, 3 vols., ed. Colin Mason. London: Oxford University Press, 1963.
3. Ferguson, Donald N. *Image and Structure in Chamber Music*. New York: Da Capo Press, 1977.
4. Kilburn, Nicholas. *Chamber Music and Its Masters in the Past and in the Present*. New York: Charles Scribner's, 1932.
5. Kirkendale, Warren. *Fugue and Fugato in Rococo and Classical Chamber Music*. Durham, NC: Duke University Press, 1979.
6. Peters, Harry B. *The Literature of the Woodwind Quintet*. Metuchen, NJ: Scarecrow Press, 1971.
7. Robertson, Alec, ed. *Chamber Music*. New York: Penguin Book, 1957.
8. Tovey, Donald Francis. *Essays in Musical Analysis; Chamber Music*. London: Oxford University Press, 1944.
9. Ulrich, Homer. *Chamber Music*, 2nd ed. New York: Columbia University Press, 1966.

Music

1. (*BH*) *Boosey & Hawkes Miniature Scores*. Oceanside, NY: Boosey & Hawkes.
2. (*EE*) *Eulenberg Miniature Scores*. New York: C. F. Peters Corporation. (Leipzig: E. Eulenberg)
3. (*IMC*) New York: International Music Company.
4. (*KSS*) *Kalmus Study Scores*. Melville, NY: Belwin-Mills Publishing Corporation.
5. (*Lea*) *Lea Pocket Scores*. Clifton, NJ: European American Music Company. (Bryn Mawr, PA: Theodore Presser Company)
6. (*PE*) *Edition Peters*. New York: C. F. Peters Corporation.
7. (*Ph*) *Philharmonia Pocket Scores*. Clifton, NJ: European American Music Company. (Vienna: Philharmonischer Verlag)

ML
161
.G522
1980

88-1931

Gramley Library
Salem College
Winston-Salem, NC 27108